Full and By

A sailing editor's word voyages through the world of sailors and sailboats

by Bill Schanen

SEAWORTHY

Seaworthy Publications
Port Washington, WI 53074

For permission to reproduce selections from this book, write to
Seaworthy Publications, 215 S. Park St., Port Washington, WI 53074

Library of Congress Cataloging-in-Publication Data

Schanen, William F., 1941-
Full and By/William F. Schanen III
p. cm.
Articles reprinted from *SAILING* Magazine
ISBN 1-892399-08-3 (pbk.: alk. paper)
1.Sailing. I. Sailing Magazine. II. Title

GV811.S28 2001

797.1'24--dc21

00-051615

Printed in the United States of America
by
Port Publications, Inc.
125 E. Main St.
Port Washington, WI 53074

Introduction

"Full and by" was a mystery to me. I was a child when I first saw the term. My father used it as the title of an editorial column he wrote for our family's weekly newspaper. I didn't have a clue as to what it meant; I doubt if many of his readers did either. I learned, of course, that it's an old sailor's expression used to describe that delightful state when a boat is sailing close to the wind with sails full.

Many years later I christened my own column in *SAILING* Magazine *Full and By*. I like to think that this monthly column of a thousand words that has appeared in more than 250 issues of the magazine has navigated the world of sailing like a boat with sails trimmed full and by, voyaging in search of sailors and sailboats, experiences and ideas to pique the interest of readers of a nautical bent.

Sailing carries a weighty freight of misperception, including the old and moldy notion that it's a rich people's game played by bluebloods in blue blazers. Funny thing, in my decades-long exploration of the sailing world looking for subjects for *Full and By*, I've come across few sailing enthusiasts who fit that stereotype. Rather, the sailors I've found are a diverse, yes, a motley, crew of dreamers, adventurers, iconoclasts, escapists, even people on a mission, not to amuse themselves, but to better mankind. The likes of the African-American who sailed alone around the world as an inspiration to inner city children to rise out of the poverty he once knew. Or the Russian who designed a radical boat for a 'round-the-world race and and sailed it to a new life of freedom in America. Or the eccentric Swede who was as much a fearless sailing adventurer as he was a brilliant inventor.

I could go on. In fact, I do on the following pages. So, let's sail away. We're going upwind. The breeze is fresh in our faces, but our sails aren't luffing ... because we're sailing full and by.

Bill Schanen
Editor and Publisher
SAILING Magazine

Contents

A Wry Look at Sailing

Polemics of Sail

On Sailboats

Sailors

A Memory of
the Last Time Around

IT was 1949, a year that hardly seems far enough back in history to be the time of freight-carrying square-riggers. People on land had television sets in their homes and automatic transmissions in their cars. But at sea, the 316-foot-long *Pamir*, with four masts, 28 sails and no engine, electricity or heat, was still relying on the wind and the strength and grit of men to deliver cargoes. When *Pamir* sailed with 60,000 bags of barley from Australia to England that year, it was the last time a cargo-carrying commercial sailing ship rounded Cape Horn.

Bill Stark remembers it as though it happened yesterday. He was aboard *Pamir* during that voyage, the lone American in a crew of 30, a band of brother Cape Horners who made a mark on the pages of sailing history.

It was the midpoint of the 20th century, but it could have been 100 years earlier. Life aboard that sailing ship was every bit the rigorous existence we armchair Cape Horners have read about in the literature of the great age of sail.

Listen to Bill Stark tell it: "Immense seas kept both the after-deck and the foredeck fully immersed with icy water. The crew clutched the lifelines with both hands. The captain and officers watched the fury from the midships deck."

That was the scene Stark encountered shortly after shipping aboard the full-rigger. He was a 22-year-old exchange student in

Europe when he heard *Pamir* was loading for a Cape Horn passage and decided on a whim to try to join her crew. He hopped a small plane to Sydney, Australia, then made his way to Port Victoria, where he worked as a stevedore on the docks where *Pamir* was moored and waited for a berth to open. A barroom brawl that sent three of the ship's regular crew to jail did the trick. Stark signed on at $200 a month.

A neophyte among seasoned sailors of the grain trade, he entered an alien world in which he slept in a dank fo'c'sle—described by Stark as lit by a single kerosene lamp, unrelentingly cold during the southern winter, smelling "of tar, sweat and oilskins"—and ate unvarying meals of salted meat, beans, dried fruit and oatmeal (though the two pigs caged on the foredeck offered the promise of fresher fare later in the voyage). On the bright side, the captain was a stern but fair Finn who took such a keen interest in the health of his crew that he personally lanced their saltwater boils with a straight razor and was liberal-minded on the subject of the consumption of rum by the sailors after a stressful watch.

Six days out, the college boy whose previous sailing had been on placid Pine Lake near his home in Wisconsin found himself climbing aloft in a gale at night, terrified and, by his admission, useless, to furl the royals on yardarms 168 feet off the deck. A burly bosun sent him on his way with a shove and a shouted insult: "This is what you signed on for—you aren't on your daddy's yacht now."

It was the beginning of what Stark described as "6,000 miles of hell," a torturous 44-day winter slog to Cape Horn through the dangerous latitudes below 40 degrees south.

"We hated the days and nights of climbing high into the screaming rigging, painfully gripping the ice-coated shrouds with raw-rubbed hands that oozed blood and pus. We were cold and wet and tired, always tired. For 11 days in a row I didn't take off my clothes. When off duty, I shucked my oilskins and dropped into my bunk."

Stark told of the crew having to bail for hours with pumps and buckets after a "40-foot sea came crashing over the ship, stoving in the messroom skylight and flooding our quarters. The lee side of the ship was under water, and the crew clung on for life."

Things got better, of course, as they always do when the sea shows her more forgiving side, and Stark reveled in a glorious sailing experience. *Pamir* rounded the Horn in comparatively quiet conditions, and the crew celebrated with bottles of rum the captain broke out for each watch. The ship turned north, the weather improved and, after 16,000 nautical miles and more than four months at sea, *Pamir* dropped her anchor in Falmouth Bay—an exclamation point at the end of an era.

With a belaying pin in his seabag, a souvenir he took with the captain's blessing, and a tear in his eye, Bill Stark left *Pamir* to finish college and return to Pewaukee, Wisconsin, to run the family candy business.

When I last spoke with him, he was thinking about traveling to Wellington, New Zealand, to attend a meeting of the Association of International Cape Horners. His *Pamir* shipmate, Murray Hendersen, harbormaster of Wellington, told him it might be the last meeting of the organization of sailing ship veterans. There aren't many Cape Horners left, and there won't be any new members. It has been half a century since the last ones, the officers and men of *Pamir*, became eligible for membership.

Immigrant on a Racing Yacht

I stepped into the surprisingly spacious cabin of the MX20, and remarked to Vlad with a wink that the 20-footer might have more headroom than the mighty *Fazisi*. He laughed a knowing laugh.

Vlad is Vladislav Murnikov, designer of both the MX20, the nimble cruiser-racer that now provides his livelihood, and the 83-foot *Fazisi*. *Fazisi* may have been the most uncomfortable Whitbread boat ever built, but that doesn't bother Vlad. She was, after all, the boat that brought him to America.

Fazisi certainly was the most interesting boat in the 1989 Whitbread Round the World Race, interesting because she came from Russia, because keeping her crew together (the first skipper committed suicide) and finding enough sponsorship money to buy groceries was an ongoing, soap operalike adventure, and because, though she finished 11th out of 23 boats, some people thought she was the fastest boat in the fleet.

Now, about the headroom. *Fazisi* below decks was a certified hellhole. Making the passage from the companionway to the bow was like crawling through a small-diameter sewer. Vlad has a ready explanation: "We had to build her of aluminum, and that was too heavy. To get rid of some weight, we cut off one foot of freeboard." This, of course, made it difficult to stand below, but Vlad maintains it wasn't that much worse than other Whitbread boats. "When the other boats piled all their sails below, they didn't have much headroom either. We were lucky—we didn't have many sails."

Even without many sails, *Fazisi*, which was in her element in the wildest surfing conditions, recorded the second longest 24-hour run in the race, 386 nautical miles.

Vlad didn't just design the boat; he organized the campaign, chased sponsors and sailed aboard for two legs, Australia to New Zealand and, most significantly, England to Fort Lauderdale, the leg that took him to his new home.

While Vlad arrived in an uncomfortable racing sailboat, his wife Tatiana and their son Pavel, then 14 years old, arrived by plane. Theirs was the more harrowing journey. "It wasn't like in the '70s and earlier when you risked your life to escape the Soviet Union but, still, it wasn't easy," Vlad says. "We didn't know where we would end up." Things were still uptight enough in Russia that Tatiana told her mother and even Pavel that they would be gone for only two weeks. But, says Vlad, "she already knew we would never come back."

The Communist empire was history by then, but Vlad has vivid memories of what it was like to be a sailor and a closet yacht designer in the old Soviet Union. "There was a lot of sailing going on, mostly in IOR racing boats, on the lakes around Moscow." Why not on the Baltic Sea or the Black Sea? Because the state did not approve. Finland and Turkey were close enough to tempt a sailor with a yen for freedom. "Boats could not even leave a seaport for a daysail without permission from the KGB, and they had to be back by sunset," Vlad says. "When there was a regatta like the Baltic Sea Cup, the KGB followed the fleet in Coast Guard boats."

Vlad, a civil architect, designed sailboats on the side. That was risky business. Engaging in private enterprise was an economic crime, the worst kind in the USSR, sometimes punishable by death, he says.

Though he got a scare when a group that asked him to design a 38-footer was investigated, he was never caught. By the time he designed *Fazisi*, things had changed enough that his work had the approval, if the not the funding, of the government.

Vlad now lives with Tatiana and Pavel in Fall River, Massachusetts, 15 minutes from the Holby Marine plant where MX20s are built. With seven sold and a number of orders pending, the boat has a good chance of being a financial success. It deserves it. The design is a clever embodiment of the fun of sailing—a sexy-looking hull with comfortable, very un*Fazisi*like accommodations for a cruising family and plenty of go-fast features, including a retractable pole for the asymmetrical spinnaker that makes the boat a reaching rocket.

Vlad still sees his adopted home country through the fresh eyes of the immigrant. It doesn't sound a bit like a cliché when he says, "A lot of people still don't realize the amount of freedom and opportunity you have here."

He expected the freedom. What caught him by surprise was the intensity of that patented American institution—competition. Trying to sell a 20-foot sport boat to buyers who are being courted by any number of other boatbuilders has been an education.

"I didn't realize the amount of competition here," he says. "In Russia it was dangerous to have initiative, but once you started you were sure to succeed because there was no competition. Here everyone wants to pursue for happiness."

True, but anyone with the moxie to start his pursuit on an 83-foot racing yacht that survived radical surgery, crew turmoil and financial disaster, not to mention the Roaring 40s, to get to the land of opportunity should have a leg up on the competition.

The Voice that Went Sailing

GLENN Yarbrough was warming to the hair-raising tale of his first ocean passage when a woman thrust a tape cassette into his hands and said, "Would you autograph this for me. I saw you at a concert in Durham, North Carolina, and your songs were the most romantic thing I ever heard."

A few minutes later, just as he was about to tell me how he came to be hanging upside down in the rigging of his boat in the Azores, a blue-jeaned couple bearing a compact disc interrupted: "We saw you in San Diego when we were in college."

And so it went, a steady stream of friendly autograph hounds making contact with a voice from the past. Glenn didn't mind the interruptions, and neither did I. He was selling tapes and CDs at a fast clip, and I was enjoying the opportunity to appraise a sampling of my generation, the source of Yarbrough's fandom. As Glenn said, "If you were in college in the '60s, you almost had to have been at a Limelighter concert." I can report that, though they seemed a bit older than I expected, my fellow college students of the 1960s are holding up well.

And so is Glenn. He's a handsome 61 now, looking sage and salty with whitening blond hair, a generous white beard and a generous body that weighs, he volunteered, something near 300 pounds. The voice—the voice that brought him celebrity, wealth and the opportunity to sail away from those attainments—is the same, pure and clear like the sound of a perfect bell. The voice that was the unmistakable trademark of the old Limelighters trio is what brought Glenn to the U.S. Sailboat Show at Annapolis. He was there, he and his girlfriend, to sell the latest Glenn Yarbrough recording, an album of sailing songs he produced himself at a cost of $50,000 because no record company would do it. If that's a comedown for a one-time superstar balladeer, it doesn't seem to bother Glenn. He traded a soaring singing career for sailing, and he considers it a fair trade.

He explained: "My idea was that singing was something you did until you grew up. I just made so much money with the Limelighters that I decided it was time to go sailing. I gave them a year's notice, then I quit."

The sailing dream formed when the Milwaukee-born Yarbrough, who had moved to the Baltimore area as a child, was a student of St. John's College in Annapolis. "I'd watch the skipjacks come to the city dock under sail. I had no idea how hard that was to do. I just thought it was beautiful."

He learned to sail on San Francisco Bay. Bothered by doubts as his departure from the Limelighters neared, he asked one of his sailing mentors what would be "the toughest thing I could do that might dissuade me from long distance sailing." The friend recommended joining a delivery crew for the return of a Transpac Race boat from Hawaii to California.

Glenn signed on a Japanese-owned boat for what would be, as his friend had predicted, a hellish voyage into high seas and headwinds punctuated by violent squalls during which, Glenn recalled, "everything broke." It took three days for him to get over his seasickness and to decide that he was exactly where he wanted to be. He learned seamanship and celestial navigation from the old paid captain. And he learned to love ocean voyaging.

Back in San Francisco, he bought a 40-year-old, 40-foot cutter built in England of teak. The boat needed work, and he did most of it, even recaulking the planks. "I was a natural at it because I'm a musician. It's all in the sound of the mallet."

Then he sailed away on a life of ocean wandering that took him more than 40,000 sailing miles and lasted, with some interruptions, for more than 20 years.

The dream and reality, of course, didn't always mesh. Wives, and there were several, who started voyages with him didn't take to sailing the way Glenn did, and so he often sailed alone, which accounts for him hanging in the rigging in Horta.

With a badly strained back, he had set sail from Bermuda, bound for the Azores. The injury rendered him virtually immobile, but the boat, an Atkin Eric gaff ketch Glenn remembers fondly for her ability to steer herself with lashed helm, needed little help. At anchor in Horta, he managed to launch the dinghy, but couldn't get himself into it. Determined not to miss a visit to Sport's bar, he hoisted himself with a block and tackle over the rail and into the dinghy. An audience of Portuguese fishermen, he said, was convulsed with laughter "by the sight of a 300-pound man hanging upsidedown from the rigging."

The injury, though, was serious. "I thought my sailing was over. I sold the boat and my sextant and charts and went back to work."

Some years later in Port Townsend, Washington, he discovered the unfinished fiberglass hull of a 34-foot Monk design. He bought it for $500, found a yard to complete the deck and interior and a handyman to install a Chinese lug rig. The boat, now lying in Friday Harbor in the San Juan Islands, is an exemplar of sailing the way Yarbrough wants it—uncomplicated. Which means no engine, no head, no through-hull fittings, no electronics and but a single bunk. He regards the latter characteristic as the boat's most attractive feature. "Wives have been my only expensive habit. This may solve that."

When he was wandering, Yarbrough would interrupt his sailing sojourns briefly to replenish the cruising kitty. His famous Coke commercial was done on one of those breaks. Recorded, he claims, in 10 minutes, it paid him $180,000 a year for three years. But for the most part Yarbrough's sailing cut him off from the recording business and television. So now, as in much of his sailing, he's going it alone with what he calls his best album. The collection of romantic sailing songs that, buoyed by the rich Yarbrough tenor, sail along like a pretty boat on a kindly sea, is entitled "I Could Have Been a Sailor."

Could have? Is he kidding? Glenn Yarbrough *is* a sailor.

Bright Ideas and Joy
in a Rough Night at Sea

IT was the closest thing to a surreal conversation I've ever had. It took place in the middle of winter during a wicked night on the Atlantic Ocean somewhere between Florida and Bermuda. The wind was roaring. The rain was coming in horizontal bullets. The seas were marching out of the night like black ghosts, flinging the boat off clifflike crests, sending her skidding into the deep troughs below. Through it all the fellow huddled next to me, tethered, as I was, to the binnacle, bracing himself against the solid seawater that regularly overwhelmed the cockpit, was engaging me in an animated, highly technical discussion of the seakeeping qualities of light-displacement sailboats designed free of the performance-numbing influence of racing rules. He did this in a lilting, Scandinavian-accented voice that rose to a high pitch to be heard over the weather din. He punctuated every point with an eye-twinkling smile. He interrupted his commentary from time to time to observe that, all things considered, it wasn't such a bad night to be sailing.

Everyone who knew Lars Bergstrom will recognize the traits that were evident that night: a scientific mind that never rested; utter fearlessness at sea; indomitable optimism.

He was an aeronautical engineer, an inventor, a designer of sailplanes and of sailboats and their rigs, appendages and equipment, an original thinker, a careful risk taker, a natural athlete

13

and a nonpareil conversationalist, all of which made him a splendid sailor. He was one of contemporary sailing's best minds.

I am, sadly, using the past tense. Lars Bergstrom is gone, killed while testing his latest motorized sailplane design in March.

Crashing in an airplane was not something you would have expected of Lars. He had flown gliders since he was a teenager in Sweden. If he seemed fearless, his wife Mary said, it was because he had a way of anticipating problems and fashioning solutions in his mind. "Then when something would happen he would just step in and calmly take care of what went wrong," she said.

Sven Ridder, his friend of 50 years, said Lars was always prepared "to do the right thing when problems came up, whether it would be a mast on the verge of collapsing or the hull leaking badly. This alertness together with unfailing courage and physical stamina enabled him to act and master situations when the rest of us were more or less paralyzed."

Ridder is the "R" in B&R Designs, the company he and Lars formed to develop some of the brightest ideas in sailing. Most of us look aloft to see their most famous one. "We tried various things," Ridder said, "but the one and only commercial success was the little wind direction indicator, Windex, now 35 years old." Many sailors, including this one, consider the Windex at the masthead, inexpensive and simple though it is, the performance instrument we would least like to sail without.

Commercial success, however, is not the standard by which Lars Bergstrom's life's work should be judged. The innovations developed by B&R, from such taken-for-granted devices as the swim platform and rigid vang to the elegantly engineered B&R rig, may not have made their developers rich but they carried sailing, which had too long been anchored by old ideas, forward.

Many of Lars' other innovations are less visible because they are under water. His keel and rudder designs, for BOC racers,

America's Cup boats, a revolutionary shorthanded cruising boat named *Route 66*, among others, all endlessly refined in the wind tunnel testing Lars believed was the essential key to sailboat design advances, made sailing faster and thus, he was convinced, better.

For a profile I wrote in 1991, Lars gave me, in surprisingly suc-cinct terms for one so voluble, his design philosophy: "Your biggest friend is speed. If you have speed, you're in control. Speed means control."

I saw Lars only once or twice a year, briefly at a boat show or some sailing event. Most of what I know of him I learned on that passage to Bermuda. You can learn a lot in six days on a small boat with someone as full of ideas and as willing to share them as was Lars. I have forgotten a good part of the hydrodynamic and aerodynamic theory he explained to me, but I will never for-get what I learned about his attitude toward sailing, which essen-tially was that it is always wonderful.

He told me of his Cape Horn voyage on *Thursday's Child* with Warren Luhrs (who sailed with us on the Bermuda run, a trip he organized to test a new boat produced by his Hunter company). It is one of his history's epic small boat passages, a 14,000-mile dash from New York around the Horn to San Francisco that broke a 135-year-old record held by a clipper ship. It was cold— for weeks on end the temperature in the cabin never got above 40 degrees Fahrenheit—and so rough that at one point the boat started breaking up. Said Lars: "It was such a delightful trip, it's hard to believe anyone would make anything of it."

He told me of how he sailed to America from England in 1968, on a 38-foot boat he designed, with a pickup crew, some of whom had never sailed before, and a sextant he didn't know how to use. Others who crossed the Atlantic at the same time complained of ter-rible conditions. To Lars, of course, "It was just a wonderful trip."

During our sail to Bermuda, much of it in foul, wintery conditions, he would frequently exclaim, "Such nice sailing."

Lars Bergstrom's legacy is secure. He will be remembered for the brilliant ideas he gave sailing.

But I'll remember him as the man who could find the joy of sailing in a miserable night at sea.

Legacy of a Chanteyman

THIS is the story of how a fast-talking New Yorker, a bit of a scamp who could be as infuriating as he was lovable, saved the South Street Seaport Museum.

The New Yorker was Bernie Klay. Without him, the South Street Seaport Museum, famed steward of American sailing heritage, might not exist at its site on historic piers in Lower Manhattan.

If that sounds like hyperbole, consider the source. Peter Stanford, the man who founded the museum, said this: "I don't think we would ever have succeeded in getting legal right to the South Street piers were it not for what Bernie did."

What Bernie did was sing sea chanteys—sailing songs that breathed life into the museum project and, in Stanford's words, "picked up something that would have failed."

It was 1968. The museum, then only a year old and more a concept than an accomplishment, was, said Stanford, who is now the president of the National Maritime Historical Society, "a squatter on the pier in an abandoned industrial wasteland, with the Fulton Fish Market occupying the ruins." Bernie showed up in Stanford's office, located in rude quarters in a weathered seaport building, and announced that he and three fellow chanteymen wanted to give a concert on the pier.

Handbills distributed by Bernie and his mates on the streets of New York brought a small group of curious people to pier 16 to hear traditional working and drinking songs of sailors sung to the accompaniment of a concertina and a guitar. It was the start of a phenomenon that grew like a wave racing to break on the shore.

Many concerts followed, and they went on for years. The 30 or 40 who gathered that first evening under the loom of the Brooklyn Bridge, beside the East River, became hundreds upon hundreds who were moved by not just the music made by Bernie and his merry group, but by the sailing life it represented.

"In a way," Stanford said, "the museum existed only when Bernie was there with his gang. Then the people he brought to the pier knew what marine history was about."

The museum went on to acquire historic ships, including the mighty bark *Peking*, to be permanently moored at the South Street piers, artifacts for its vast collection displayed in a series of seaport buildings and a sterling reputation. Bernie Clay made a name for himself too.

Holder of a civil engineering degree, he was manager of maintenance for the New York City school system when he developed an interest in folk art and dancing. On a visit to Newport, Rhode Island, he was introduced to the folk art of sea chanteys and, according to Peter Stanford, "it dragged on his soul."

Bernie formed the group that would be known as the X-Seamen's Institute and became a tireless sea chantey evangelist, awakening the South Street crowds to the richness of their sailing heritage and the music that grew out of it and spurring a resurging interest in traditional maritime music across the country. The X-Seamen's numerous recorded collections represent an extensive library of historic sailing songs, from the essential chanteys, the likes of "Drunken Sailor" and "Rio," to bawdy ditties, heart-tugging sailors' ballads and the heroic verses of "Heart of Oak."

I never heard the X-Seamen in person. (What I would have given to be at one of those South Street concerts when, as Peter Stanford put it, "people gathered as the sky darkened, and then the piers came to life.") But I talked with Bernie enough (and at considerable length, which was the norm when conversing with the loquacious one, as his long-listening acquaintances would attest) to recognize his voice on the X-Seamen's tapes. As Stanford observed, "Bernie had a sort of croaky voice, but he made it work." Did he ever. It is just the sort of sailorly voice, touched with a rough edge as though worn by too much shouting above the gale, that you would expect to hear leading the tars in the foc's'le in a sailing song, whether rousing or mournful.

Sea chantey singing was but one chapter in Bernie's eventful life story. Among many others, he founded the Sea Heritage Foundation, edited a lively newspaper called the Sea Heritage News and turned his prodigious energy to promoting the work of a British marine artist named John Stobart, once little known in the United States, now the pre-eminent name in marine art.

About his infuriating side, a longtime friend noted that Bernie had "multitudinous critics." The words "audacious" and "abrasive" are standard adjectives in any Bernie story. True to his Brooklyn upbringing, when he focused on doing something, he applied sufficient chutzpah and just did it, sorting out the consequences or, as was often the case, the financial accounting, later. It was how he operated. To his friends, who were legion, it was a fair price to pay for the pleasure of knowing him.

Bernie, whose complete and proper name was Bernard Klayman and who was often called Commodore, died last July at the age of 75. At the orthodox Jewish burial ceremony, as his mourners filed by for the ritual tossing of a shovel of dirt into the grave, one of Bernie's chantey-singing acolytes struck up a song. And then spontaneously the voices of the many who had gathered to see him off to Fiddler's Green joined in singing "Pleasant and Delightful," the old sailing song with which Bernie always ended his concerts.

A fit farewell for a savior of some of our sailing heritage.

We Can't Say 'Mike Always Makes It' Anymore

WHEN I spoke with Rodger Martin recently to check some details for a column I was wrapping up, he mentioned that Mike Plant had not been heard from since he reported a few days earlier that his boat had lost electrical power. Martin, Plant's friend and designer of the boat he was sailing singlehanded across the Atlantic, wasn't overly concerned.

At about the same time in Les Sables d'Olonne, France, members of Mike's shore crew, aware that he had a problem, were impatient: He would probably arrive later than planned; they would have less time to prepare the boat for the start of the Vendée Globe Challenge around-the-world race. But they weren't particularly worried.

I had no qualms about writing then that Plant is "now" racing around the world. It never crossed my mind that he wouldn't make it to the start of the race.

Rodger Martin spoke for many when he said, "Most of us made the mistake of thinking that Mike always makes it."

He always did, no matter what.

In three singlehanded races around the world, he had experienced capsize, collision, dismasting, equipment failures and killer storms, and he always made it.

Jeremy McGeary, Plant's friend and shore crew member, said, "I couldn't believe there was anything Mike couldn't handle."

In the end, there was.

"When the bulb came off the keel, it was the only situation he couldn't deal with," McGeary said.

They found the boat—the exotic Open Class 60 named *Coyote*—460 miles north of the Azores on the day the Globe race started, floating keel up, the four and one-half ton ballast bulb missing. A group of Mike's friends, including his fiance Helen Davis, were watching the start, on television and through the window of their hotel room in Les Sables d'Olonne, when word came from the Coast Guard that the boat had been sighted by a tanker.

There was hope then, even as there had been earlier when signals were received from *Coyote's* EPIRB that Mike, as always, would somehow make it. Three days later divers found a life raft and a survival suit on the capsized boat but no sign of Mike, and everyone knew that this time he wasn't going to make it.

The aftermath of this sailing tragedy is weighted with surmise and supposition; scenarios abound. One is that the capsize was almost instant, violent enough to throw a man overboard, with almost no chance in heavy seas to dive under and into the hull to find the refuge of trapped air.

If the boat is salvaged—an uncertain possibility at this writing—there may be clues to what caused the bulb to separate from the spar-like carbon fiber keel. So far, there are only theories. And talk.

There is talk that the *Coyote* program was so rushed, that the weeks before the departure from New York were so chaotic, that the voyage was fated to end badly.

True, the launching was late; the "things to do" list were daunting; Mike was under pressure. But, nothing unusual there, nothing Mike hadn't handled before.

The power failure, as Rodger Martin put it, was "a nasty problem." But he had every expectation Mike would fix it, as he had said he would do when he raised a freighter on his hand-held VHF radio.

That radio transmission adds a poignant footnote to the story. While Mike was speaking, the freighter captain placed a single sideband radiotelephone call to Helen Davis in France, and she was able to hear what was to be his last communication.

The power problem was nasty because without the 24 and 12 volt electricity (generated by two hand-start engines with separate fuel supplies), Mike was deprived of electronic navigation, long distance radio contact and, worst, his autopilots. *Coyote*, 60 feet long, ultra light, with an enormous rig, was a lot for one man to handle without self-steering capability. Yet it was something Mike could do.

Both Martin and McGeary describe him as a careful, skilled seaman. McGeary recalled that while sailing *Coyote* from Annapolis to New York with a crew, including McGeary, aboard, it was a conservative Mike Plant who insisted that sail area be reduced when the weather breezed up.

The mundane details of putting the boat together, of rigging, tuning, installing equipment and provisioning, must have seemed a pleasure compared to the ongoing challenge of financing the project. Lack of adequate sponsorship lent a certain "under the gun" mood to the final days.

It was the distracting search for funding that sent *Coyote* and her skipper to the Annapolis Sailboat Show in October and then back to New York instead directly across the Atlantic. Aboard *Coyote* when she foundered were hundreds of sweatshirts, printed with the green *Coyote* logo, intended to be sold to help pay the bills.

The shirts would sell well in France, Helen said at Annapolis. Indeed they would have. The French regarded Mike, like all the great professional sailors, as a sports hero. The search for him was front page news in France. In the U.S., it was barely news at all. No surprise there. Few Americans had ever heard of their countryman who in Europe was a famous singlehanded ocean racing sailor.

Billy Black, the photographer whose splendid images often appear in sailing magazines, had tried for years without success to sell the story of Mike Plant to the mainstream press. When *Coyote* was found, *Sports Illustrated* sent a courier to France, where Billy waited with Mike's friends, to pick up his transparencies for a seven-page spread on the world class athlete who wasn't judged newsworthy until he disappeared in the North Atlantic.

Born in the Breezes

COME April 24, 1995, it would be fitting for us sailors to take a moment from our Monday's duties to reflect on our good fortune. It is our good fortune to have Joshua Slocum. We have him in the firm embrace of our lore, our history and our ethic. We are fortunate because no one before or since his stunning achievement has been better qualified to be the exemplar of small boat sailors. His achievement was to be the first to sail alone around the world. He was the best of all sailors to make this bold mark in history because he combined surpassing seafaring skill, courage and an unquenchable love of the sea with a rare ability to translate his experiences into words. For the latter, especially, we who sail a century after Slocum began his epic voyage—it will be exactly 100 years on that date in April—should be thankful. His book **Sailing Alone Around the World** remains a literate, entertaining and inspirational story that turns on the irresistible allure of sailing.

That Slocum could write such a book is as astonishing as his sailing feat. He was born on a rugged Nova Scotian island and went to sea at 16 without any formal education. "I was born in the breezes," he wrote with his typical flair for compelling language," and I had studied the sea as perhaps few men have studied it, neglecting all else."

By the age of 25 he was a captain, commanding the first of a succession of barks and ships until, in the dusk of the clippership era near the end of the 19th century, he found himself on the beach, broke, without a ship to sail.

"What was there for an old sailor to do?" he asked in **Sailing Alone**. The answer, of course, was—go sailing. And this he did after rebuilding an ancient oyster dredging sloop given to him by a whaling captain. *Spray* was a clunky looking boat, 37 feet long, heavy, shallow, broad-sterned. Slocum was 51, described by a newspaper reporter on the eve of his departure as "a kinky salt, five feet nine and one-half inches tall, weighing 146 pounds, spry as a kitten and nimble as a monkey."

You know about the voyage. If not, I envy you; the pleasure of reading **Sailing Alone** is still ahead. Slocum sailed west around the world, 46,000 miles in three years and two months. His passage in gales through the Strait of Magellan inside of Cape Horn, one of the great feats of sailing history, has been compared to the exploits of Magellan and Drake. His escape from the rock-strewn trap called the Milky Way is one of the most harrowing sea stories you will ever read. Slocum called it his "greatest sea adventure."

Accounts of Slocum's adventures had preceded his return to America, and an enthusiastic audience awaited publication of his book, which became a best seller and made the flinty sailor an unlikely celebrity. Reviewers were kind, one referring to Slocum as "a stylist and a wit." He was that. He managed to tell of his hair-raising adventures and communicate the splendor of sailing the oceans without taking himself too seriously. After reporting that at one point during his terrible time in the Magellan Strait he had no appetite for his usual hearty meal of venison stew or the like, he wrote in parenthesis: "Confidentially, I was seasick."

Just as in these cynical times, Slocum's celebrity made him an inviting target for doubters. Some said his account of sailing for days without touching the wheel of *Spray* had to be a lie. Why, I can't imagine. With her long keel, firm bilges and the yawl rig

Slocum added during the voyage, she was a prime candidate to steer herself. Besides, Slocum could hardly have stayed at the helm for 46,000 miles.

The very excellence of **Sailing Alone** invited charges, even long after Slocum's death, that it had been ghostwritten. In *SAILING*'s archives I found a copy of a letter, published in the *National Fisherman* in 1965, in which Howard I. Chapelle, the much respected curator of transportation of the Smithsonian, claimed the words in Slocum's book "are not his but are a ghost-writer's, for the captain was hardly literate as his letters show." Obviously no fan of the Slocum legend, Chapelle in the same letter called *Spray* "a damned bucket."

Chapelle could have been right about *Spray*, but not about Slocum, the writer. Slocum certainly had an editor. His letters show he wasn't the greatest speller and had an odd habit of omitting periods at the end of sentences. But his letters also reveal that he could turn a phrase. There is no evidence that the language in his book isn't his. The well-read, self-educated seaman was a natural writer. **Sailing Alone**, in fact, was not his first book. After his second most remarkable sailing adventure, a passage in 1889 from Brazil to New York with his wife and two sons in a 35-foot canoe-type sailboat he built, he wrote and published **Voyage of the Liberdade**. I have never seen the book, but one of Slocum's biographers, Walter Teller, wrote that it was a good piece of work.

Slocum had money enough from book sales to buy a farm on Martha's Vineyard. His admirers were legion; he had entree to New York society. Yet he was also, like so many seafarers on shore, a fish out of water. "Almost from the minute the voyage ended, Slocum felt desperately idle and unemployed," Teller wrote.

His remedy, of course, was to go sailing. He and *Spray* made several uneventful voyages to the West Indies. In November,

1909, they set sail again for Slocum's favorite winter port of Grand Cayman, and were never seen again.

The disappearance of Joshua Slocum was a mystery, but not a tragedy. Slocum, at the age of 65, died sailing. A tragedy would have been for this magnificent sailor to have died any other way.

We remember him with fondness and more than a touch of awe during this year of the Joshua Slocum Centennial.

Solo but Not Alone

BILL Pinkney bristles a bit when someone observes that there aren't many black recreational sailors.

While conceding that yacht club yearbook photos are not exactly filled with black faces, Pinkney points out that the forebears of American blacks played a more important role in the earliest American sailing history than the ancestors of those traditional yacht club types.

"In the Revolutionary War," Pinkney says, "almost all of the pilots were slaves because they were watermen. Blacks were captains, mates, even ship owners. They were our best sailors. How the hell do you think people got up and down the west coast of Africa? They didn't take a bus."

But talking about long gone black sailors is a distraction for Pinkney. He'd rather talk about today's kids, black, brown and white ones, inner city kids whose prospects are limited by their desperate surroundings. For them, Bill Pinkney is sailing alone around the world.

It will be many months before the thousands of schoolchildren who are following his odyssey and the rest of us know whether he was successful, whether he even survived. But we can say now that few, if any, sailors have embarked on a seafaring adventure for more noble reasons than Bill Pinkney. People have sailed around the world for the challenge—because the oceans are there—to make history, to make money, to gain fame. Pinkney is doing it for the kids.

"I want to teach an object lesson to inner city kids," he explains. "I'm saying, 'Look what you can do.'

"I want to show these kids that you can set a goal and accomplish it, that you can be a real person, that you don't have to be a TV stereotype.

"I want to show them that you can reach goals if you sacrifice, if you're willing to pay a price, a price, as in my case, of solitude, fear, perseverance and disappointment—God knows I have had enough of that raising money for this project."

Raising money for his object lesson has been a full time job for Pinkney for the last three years, which hasn't left a lot of time for sailing. In fact, as circumnavigators go, Pinkney is light on experience.

His saltwater sailing experience consists of some racing in schooners and a delivery from the East Coast to the Virgins. On Lake Michigan he sailed in seven Chicago-Mackinac Races and some shorthanded races. He has a 100-ton Coast Guard captain's license.

Pinkney is not daunted by the risky test he faces. "We've all got to make some sort of peace with our own mortality," he philosophizes.

Relative peace is what he expects to find at sea on his 27,000-mile voyage (which with eight or nine stops is expected to take almost a year) after the hectic years he spent persuading more than 30 companies and foundations to sponsor his circumnavigation-for-the-kids. The experience has left him with the conviction that "raising money is a hell of a lot more difficult than sailing."

Pinkney won't be the first American to sail alone around the world (though, surprisingly, there have been only three), nor the first black. Virgin Islander Ted Seymour, who completed his circumnavigation in 1987, has that honor. But he'll probably be the first beauty school graduate to do it, which tells us something about Bill Pinkney's ability to be successful at the things he does.

Born 54 years ago in the south side Chicago neighborhood that was then called Bronzeville, the kind of place the kids he's sailing for call home, he has served on U.S. Navy ships, including a battleship and aircraft carrier, as a hospital X-ray technician. He has worked as an elevator mechanic and a limbo dancer, as a bartender and as a hand on Caribbean freight sloops. He did, indeed, graduate from beauty school, after which he excelled as a makeup artist for such entertainers as Red Buttons, Roberta Flack and Jaclyn Smith, then was recruited by Revlon, where he became its first black executive. He later developed cosmetic products at another firm, produced promotional films and became a sought after motivational speaker. He's married and has a daughter and two grandchildren.

Besides buying the boat (a Valiant 47 sailed in the 1987 BOC by Mark Schrader) and furnishing equipment, Pinkney's sponsors are funding the educational program that is the heart of this unique effort. School children in Chicago, Los Angeles and other cities will be part of the voyage via satellite links to computer networks. They will not only follow Pinkney's progress but will work on lessons relevant to the voyage in oceanography, astronomy, meteorology, geography, history and social studies.

But the most important lesson Bill Pinkney wants his audience of inner city children to learn is painted on the transom of his boat, which he named *Commitment*.

"When a young black person sees that a black man, by making a commitment and the sacrifices that go with it, can circle the globe alone in a small boat, can she or he feel that anything less is not in reach?" he asks.

Does this mean he sees himself as a role model?" No. I don't want all these kids running out to sail around the world. That's really a pretty dumb thing to do. There's a lot of more important things for them to do."

Perhaps, but there is no more important thing for Bill Pinkney to do. By doing it he is, if not a role model, a shining example of a brave and determined sailor who, like those early African-Americans who sailed in the Revolutionary War, happens to be black.

His Dream Came True
in a Nightmare Boat

DO you wonder why a sailboat is a she? These exquisite objects we sailors love too much can be heartbreakers. Our expectations are so high, our dreams so perfect: Our boats will be fast yet forgiving, strong yet graceful, beautiful yet formidable enough to defeat the fiercest seas. The dreams of sailors come with guarantees against boats that are cranky, clumsy, unresponsive, slow, hard to manage or aesthetically disappointing. Reality comes with no guarantees.

Francis Chichester dreamed of the boat he would sail to glory. "I used to lie awake at night," he wrote, "imagining her steering down the faces of the great Southern Ocean rollers ... going so fast that she would be able to challenge the great runs of the clippers."

Chichester did sail to glory, but with no thanks to the boat of his dreams. His sailing records should be marked with asterisks to indicate that they are even more than they seem because they were made in one of the most abominable vessels to which a singlehander ever entrusted his life.

In May of 1967 he completed his grandest adventure, a voyage around the world that was twice as fast as any circumnavigation.

Chichester was a born adventurer, a gold prospector, boxer and daring aviator at a young age; winner of the first single-handed transatlantic race by the time, at a rather ripe age, that he set off to break the around-the-world record. He went to the renowned English naval architect, John Illingworth, for the boat that would be *Gipsy Moth IV*, named after the airplane in which, as a young man, he tried unsuccessfully to fly around the world.

How Chichester's heart must have ached when he first raised the sails on Illingworth's design. His dream boat did not merely disappoint him; she frightened a brave man. He wrote: "The thought of what she would do in the huge Southern Ocean seas put ice into my blood."

On her first sail, on a calm Solent, *Gipsy Moth* was knocked flat—spars parallel to the water—by a meager 20-knot puff. Ballast was added, but the boat remained so tender that Chichester endured thousands of miles of windward sailing heeled at a 35-40 degree angle. In spite of her tippiness, she need-ed all of her complicated sail plan set to make respectable speed in moderate wind. Chichester was constantly setting and hand-ing the sails of a 10-sail ketch rig—without the benefit of roller furling. Chichester had counted on the weatherliness of the rela-tively narrow 54-footer to maintain record-setting speed through windward passages, but when pointing high *Gipsy Moth* would hobby-horse to a standstill. Chichester had to steer the boat so far off the wind that he reckoned he was pointing at about the same absurdly broad beating angle as the clipperships that preceded him almost a century earlier.

Judging from what Chichester wrote in his book, **Gipsy Moth Circles the World**, he managed to be quite cheerful, amazingly calm through it all. He expressed about as much concern over capsizing in the Tasman Sea as a malfunction in the tapping sys-tem of his beloved keg of Whitbread's. Still, the voyage was an ordeal.

Chichester's travail seems all the more excruciating when compared to the experience of an American who, 20 years after

Chichester, set the record for fastest solo non-stop circumnavigation. Dodge Morgan's remarkable feat—150 days around the world—involved risk, a good deal of angst over the long separation from his family and contrary weather but little of the physical suffering of Chichester's trial. The difference was the boat; *American Promise* measured up to Morgan's dream.

A powerful representation of Ted Hood's heavy displacement solution to boat speed, the 60-foot *Promise* was an engineering and electronic marvel with layers of redundancy to keep complex systems working so that Morgan could sail the boat from below deck or the deep, covered cockpit.

The physical demands of *American Promise* were so restrained that Morgan began doing daily exercises to control the spare tire that appeared on his midriff. That was hardly Chichester's problem. He wasted away, unable to keep his nourishment up to the demands his quirky boat made on his body. Morgan, who comes across in his book, **The Voyage of American Promise**, as bluff and boisterous, underwent a psychological evaluation that pronounced him well qualified for his voyage owing to a high quotient of something called "tough-poise." The most that Chichester, the taciturn Englishman, would reveal about his psyche was, "I hate being frightened, but, even more, I detest being prevented by fright."

Fear was not his problem. Indeed, he is remembered most of all for his astonishing courage. At his single port of call, he was welcomed as a hero by an adoring—and worried—public. Chichester arrived in Sydney in wretched condition, lame, looking frail and starved. Photos published in English newspapers, especially one of the tired sailor being hugged by his son, appalled readers. Chichester lamented in a poignant passage, "He is much taller than I am, and pretty husky, and the photograph makes me look like an old man of a hundred weeping on his shoulder."

Friends, fearing he would not survive Cape Horn on the return leg, implored Chichester not to go on. Captain Alan Villiers, redoubtable veteran of Cape Horn roundings as master of full-rigged sailing ships, told a journalist: "I beg Chichester not to attempt it. I don't know what drives this man to go on tempting the might of the seas."

Driven he was. The undaunted Chichester sailed on and 119 days later arrived in England, battered but triumphant. After a month in the hospital, he was knighted by the sword of a sailor he resembled in name and fortitude—Sir Francis Drake.

The achievement would have been no less inspiring had it been accomplished by a rugged 25-year-old, but it adds laurels to his memory to recall that the slight, bespectacled Chichester celebrated his 65th birthday while sailing alone around the world in a boat that would have given fits to a crew of eight.

Novels for Sailors
who 'Love a Blow'

IF I would have written this when I read my first Patrick O'Brian sailing book in 1990, I might have been hailed as a visionary, perhaps embraced as a prescient darling of the nautical literati. But instead of writing about him, I kept reading him, one book after another, pressed into service by the force of O'Brian's irrestible tales to sail thousands of ocean miles with Lucky Jack Aubrey and Dr. Stephen Maturin. I make no claim of discovering O'Brian; when I happened onto **Master and Commander**, the first book of the Aubrey-Maturin series, the story was 20 years old, though it had just been published in the U.S. Still, I feel like the first person on the block to own a VCR or a microwave, because Patrick O'Brian, an obscure Irish writer of historical novels when I first came across his work, is suddenly famous. At age 80, he has arrived at literary stardom. The publication of his latest book, **The Wine-Dark Sea**, last October inspired a lovefest among American critics and literary pundits, a number of whom could not resist declaring, "His ship has come in."

Well, we should be proud—he's one of us. Patrick O'Brian is a sailor. It's what makes his stories of 19th century seafaring so compelling. This man, you can tell from his precisely crafted language, knows the sea, sailors and sailboats. He went sailing on the Irish Sea as a child, often on a bark-rigged merchantman owned by a friend of his family. There, O'Brian told an interviewer, he learned to hand, reef and steer in the manner of the square-riggers.

He augmented his sailing knowledge with painstaking research into the minutiae of Nelson's navy by reading ship's logs, the preserved letters of sailors of the 1700s and 1800s, memoirs and naval history. O'Brian obviously takes delight—sometimes I think a perverse delight—in sharing what he learned with his readers. Think you know your sailing terms? Then what do you make of this account of the refitting of the sloop *Sophie*?" ... brace-pendants were rigged after the horses, after the stirrups, after the yard-tackle pendants or a thimble for the tackle-hook."

Not that O'Brian takes this too seriously. The esoteric nature of the nomenclature of a sailing ship is an ongoing joke in the series. Maturin, a physician who can recite the name and precise location of every bone and organ in the human body and a naturalist who can classify virtually any species, is baffled by his friend's sailing lingo.

It is safe to say, though, that it is not the challenge of deciphering arcane sailing terms that has persuaded readers to buy more than 600,000 O'Brian books since W.W. Norton & Company did Americans a favor and began publishing them in 1990. It's the stories, made-up adventures rooted in historical fact, told in beautifully turned prose and enlivened by a literary duo far more complex, interesting and likable than others that come to mind, including Don Quixote and Sancho Panza and Holmes and Watson.

Jack Aubrey is every sailor's hero. He rose through the ranks, made the hard journey from the ordinary seaman's world before the mast back to the quarterdeck, where captains walk. As fearless in battle as he is in the face of a Cape Horn gale, he is a warrior and a charismatic leader but most of all he is a consummate sailor. He resembles nothing so much as a canny racing skipper who can't resist tweaking and trimming until he satisfied himself his boat can sail no faster. His exhilaration when the ship is in tune with the wind and sea is something sailors understand, as is his embarrassment when his crew botches an anchoring maneuver before the assembled fleet.

His partner Dr. Maturin, though a poor sailor, is the intellectual superior of Aubrey and is as formidable in his disciplines—stitching wounds, amputating limbs and performing operations, including rather frequent brain surgery, at sea and gathering intelligence ashore for the war against Napoleon—as the captain is in his.

These heroes of O'Brian's are more accessible than most, thanks to a realistic streak of human frailty. Maturin, given to dark depressions, finds relief drinking self-prescribed opium tincture and chewing coca leaves. Big, bluff Jack is in full possession of the sailorly weaknesses. He is wont to drink and eat to excess—Dr. Maturin nags him for being florid and overweight; surely he has high blood pressure and a cholesterol count that is off the chart—and early in the series is treated by Maturin for what was once politely called a social disease.

O'Brian's sailing novels are adventure stories, but hardly potboilers. The reader is asked to interrupt the furious page turning frequently to keep track of digressions from the narrative that seem to amuse the author. O'Brian, in fact, is a master of digression. Aubrey's gallant frigate *Surprise* may be bearing down on an enemy ship for a climactic battle, but that doesn't stop Maturin from launching into an involved discourse on the mating habits of a seabird he has just identified. A ferocious storm may be building, but Aubrey finds time to join Maturin in the captain's cabin to play (Aubrey on the violin, Maturin the cello) the works of an obscure Italian composer. Longer digressions take us on shore where Jack invariably makes a fool of himself dealing with creditors or the Byzantine politics of the English navy. Just as this is about to get tiresome, O'Brian takes us back where we want to be, on deck beside Jack Aubrey, reveling in the majesty of a sailing ship riding a gale: "...the frigate was racing along under a press of canvas, lying over so that her deck sloped like a roof and her lee chains were buried in the foam; twelve and a half knots with the wind on her quarter—royals, upper and lower studdingsails, almost everything she had ... vast smooth waves, dark, mottled with white, running from the west diagonally across the frigate's course, two hundred yards from crest to crest."

Maturin beholds the ocean's power and remarks, "It is grandiose."

"Ain't it?" said Jack. "I do love a blow."

Norton has published all 20 books of O'Brian's Aubrey-Maturin series. So, if you love a blow, you can sail a long way with Jack Aubrey.

Shackleton's Cold Sail
into History

I HAVE not climbed Mt. Everest. However, I have gone ice fishing.

Which means I know something about being cold. Standing motionless on 2-foot-thick ice, rasped by the subzero wind, waiting for a fish (lucky fellow in his sheltered liquid environment) to make a mistake that will jiggle a pole tip or flip a tip-up, is cold work. Still, the coldest feeling place on earth that I have visited is not a godforsaken frozen lake but the cockpit of a sailboat. In certain latitudes at certain times of the year, sailing, with a similar dearth of opportunity to generate body heat aerobically, has much in common with ice fishing. The main difference is that it's much easier to escape ice fishing: Pull up your gear and head for a cozy saloon. Sailing, you're in it for the duration of the passage.

All of that said, I pledge to never again complain about being cold while sailing. I decided to make this oath after reading **Endurance: Shackleton's Incredible Voyage**, which I believe is one of the greatest, not to mention one of the coldest, sailing stories ever told.

I'm a little surprised that I didn't read it until 39 years after it was published. When the book, handsomely written by the late Alfred Lansing in a restrained prose that uses facts gleaned from logbooks, diaries and survivor interviews to tell a story of intense drama, came out, I was in high school, inhaling every scrap of sailing literature I could find. By then I had read **Two Years Before the Mast** three times, but somehow had never heard of this Shackleton tale. It turns out that my tardy discovery coincides with that of Hollywood and business management gurus. Now there's a Shackleton movie in the works and something called "the Shackleton way" that is used as a model for corporate leadership—83 years after Sir Ernest Shackleton carried off his incredible feat.

Shackleton was the prototypical British adventurer, brave to a fault, greedy for glory and the rewards of the post-adventure lecture circuit, which he aimed to acquire by hiking 1,500 miles across the Antarctic continent. He failed, but in dealing with his failure he revealed himself as one of history's extraordinary leaders and a sailor for the ages.

To get in position for the crossing, the 40-year-old Shackleton and his party of 27 sailed the barkentine *Endurance* into the Weddell Sea—and promptly got stuck in the ice 1,200 miles southeast of Cape Horn. Like castaways on a tiny island, Shackleton and his crew lived for months on the trapped ship until it was finally squeezed to pieces by the ice. Then they survived on an ice floe, buoyed through periods of ghastly weather by the indomitable optimism of the man they called "the boss." When the floe broke up, they took to three open boats they had salvaged from *Endurance*, and began a perilous voyage through a sea that was more ice than water. After days of misery, rowing and sailing in appalling conditions, they managed to land on a rocky shelf of a beach confined by cliffs on Elephant Island. That was the easy part. A sterner survival test awaited.

Shackleton decided to sail for help in one of the boats with five of his men. No voyage I know of, with the possible exception of the one that faced William Bligh after he was put off the *Bounty* and into an overloaded longboat, has ever had the odds stacked more heavily against it. Consider:

The sea conditions Shackleton and his men faced in the waters around latitude 60 south were the most dangerous in the world. We know about them from accounts of Whitbread, Vendée Globe and BOC sailors who have ventured near, though never as far south, as Shackleton's starting point.

Their boat was manifestly unfit for such a challenge. The *James Caird* (named after a sponsor, even in 1914), about as long as a Star boat and just over 6 feet wide, was an open, double-ended whaleboat with a stumpy yawl rig. Though the ship's carpenter attempted to partially enclose the boat with dogsled runners and canvas, there was little protection from weather so cold the crew had to chip ice off the rig and hull to avoid capsizing.

Their destination was South Georgia Island, only 25 miles wide, nearly 1,000 miles away.

They made it, no doubt because Shackleton willed that they make it. But if the leader was exceptional, so were his followers. The men on the *Caird* displayed a resistance to despair that seems beyond human capability. Always soaked, in temperatures that were always below freezing and sometimes below zero, they endured—not only without shelter but without even adequate clothing. They wore woolen pants and sweaters, gabardine over-alls and worn-out reindeer boots. "There was not," Lansing wrote, "a set of oilskins on board."

And without Frank Worsley, I wouldn't be writing about Ernest Shackleton. Worsley, a professional sailor from New Zealand, was the navigator on whom fell the enormous burden of finding a speck in the ocean. Had he failed, they would have perished. After South Georgia, the next stop was Africa, 3,000 miles away. Worsley's *Nautical Almanac* was soaked to a barely readable pulp. The sun was rarely visible. He had to be held by two men on the helmsman's seat of the heaving boat to attempt to get a sight. Yet he guided them to a landfall on South Georgia Island.

On South Georgia, Shackleton commandeered a whaling ship and was able to penetrate the ice surrounding Elephant Island and rescue his crew. Like the crew of the *Caird*, everyone on the beach survived. Shackleton didn't lose a single man.

As a footnote to the Shackleton sailing story, here is a Shackleton mountaineering story: The point where the *Caird* made its harrowing landing on South Georgia was some 130 sea miles from the island's whaling station, and neither the exhausted crew nor the boat was up to the passage. Shackleton decided to hike across the mountainous island. With Worsley and another sailor, a carpenter's adze and 50 feet of line, he did just that, a feat that was thought impossible at the time and wasn't accomplished again until 40 years later, by a fully rigged mountain climbing expedition.

One of his crew was to write later: " ... when you are in a hopeless situation, when there seems no way out, get down on your knees and pray for Shackleton."

Amen.

The Greatest English Sailor was Not a Screamer

HAVE you noticed how loud this quiet sport of ours often is?

On many boats a sail cannot be set, a mark rounded, or a slip entered without someone hollering.

Only in sailing is there a sweatshirt designed for verbally battered crew persons with a legend that admonishes, "Don't yell at me!"

Well, here is something for you screamers, for you martinets, you wanna-be Captain Blighs to think about: England's—perhaps the world's—greatest sailing hero ran his ships not with the lash but with love. Vice Admiral Horatio Viscount Nelson—Lord Nelson, who destroyed Napoleon's navy at Trafalgar—commanded men hardened by the brutal life of the British navy with kindness, respect and a calm voice.

"He is remembered not mainly because he was a great admiral, a great tactician, or even a great hero in the military sense—but because he was an exceptionally kind and lovable man."

The words are from a wonderful biography by David and Steven Howarth entitled **Lord Nelson: The Immortal Memory**.

As they trace this remarkable life, the Howarths, father and son, return time and again to the love that bound Nelson to his officers and men and was surely the inspiration for the astonishing courage they displayed in battle after battle.

Nelson called the officers of his fleet his "band of brothers." He treated them as equals and imparted his brilliant and quite unconventional instructions for battle not in orders but in free ranging discussions over wine and dinner aboard his ship. After one such dinner, a veteran ship's captain wrote to his wife that he was moved to tears by the warmth and affection Nelson displayed.

Nelson was loath to have men flogged aboard his ships, though it was the commonest form of discipline in the British navy. On shore he shirked his duty to preside at the execution of a deserter. Shortly before his last battle, at Trafalgar, Nelson called back a ship that was sailing for England with mail to pick up a single letter a boatswain's mate had written his wife but forgot to put in the mail bag.

"Men adored him," one sailor wrote, "and in fighting under him every man thought himself sure of success."

If they adored him for his kindness, they respected him for his courage. As he went into the battle of Trafalgar, Nelson, at age 47, had lost an arm and eye in battle, carried the scar of a serious head wound and was wracked by the effects of tropical diseases contracted during his service in the West Indies. He stood resolutely on the quarterdeck of *HMS Victory* as she sailed slowly toward the line of French ships, her gunners observing Nelson's order to hold fire until *Victory* struck the stern of a French ship. This diminutive figure, barely five and a half feet tall, empty sleeve dangling, stood exposed, unflinching in a hail of grapeshot, cannonballs and musket fire. Men would follow such a captain anywhere.

It was not always easy following Nelson. *Victory* was at sea blockading the French fleet for two years before the battle of Trafalgar. Her crew of 847 endured vile weather, the cramped, soggy, odoriferous, cold life aboard a 200-foot ship, which included foul drinking water and salt meat so hard it was carved into ship's models, yet when the French put to sea Nelson's men were ready to chase them twice across the Atlantic.

For his part, Nelson was as good at sailing as he was at fighting. A consummate seaman, Nelson learned to sail as a boy among the shifting sand bars and dangerous tides of the estuaries of the coast of England. He so valued a ship's sailing ability that for a long time he insisted on keeping command of the lightly armed but swift *Agamemnon* rather than moving his flag to the larger, more prestigious but ponderous ships of the line that were offered him. His contrarian battle strategy, which eschewed the accepted practice of lining up parallel to the enemy fleet and, dead in the water, blasting away, was based on maneuvering adeptly through the enemy's line and put a premium on the English crews' ability to sail.

Though he was chronically seasick, Nelson was a better person at sea than on land. Ashore he was dogged by a scandalous love affair, lack of money and a foolish vanity that seemed to surface the moment his foot hit land. At sea, he was a sailor for the ages.

His victory at Trafalgar was so complete that it effectively ended naval warfare for a century, yet to the men of the English navy in 1805, indeed to all of England, the victory paled beside its price, the life of Horatio Nelson.

The Howarths write: "When he died at Trafalgar, his fleet forgot its victory in an astonishing spontaneous outburst of grief: the commander they had lost seemed more important to them than the triumph they had won."

In the choking aftermath of the battle, a sailor on the still smoky gundeck wrote home: "Our dear Admiral Nelson is killed … Chaps that fought like the devil sit down and cry like a wench."

It is not recorded who cried when William Bligh died 12 years after Nelson, but among those who sailed under him his mourners were probably relatively few. In spite of the revisionist history improving his image on the 200th anniversary of the mutiny on the *Bounty*, it is safe to say Bligh was not one to inspire love.

Nor was he the monster Charles Laughton made him in the first *Bounty* movie. By most accounts he was a fair and humane captain. By every account he was an extremely capable seaman and a brilliant navigator whose 3,618-mile voyage in an open launch from the site of the *Bounty* mutiny to the island of Timor is one of the great sea odysseys.

The flaw in this contemporary of Nelson was a rotten temper. When angered, his ability to heap profane, vitriolic insult on subordinates was so impressive that one observer likened an outburst to a flogging—"verbal lashing," he called it. It eventually cost Bligh his ship.

Bligh was a screamer.

An Inspiration from the Slingshot Age

COMPETITORS in the Around Alone Race regularly send photos by e-mail—digital images transmitted through cyberspace by laptop computers tied to a satellite communications system.

We are no longer astonished, or even surprised by this sort of thing. But here's a measure of how far we've come: In the first-ever singlehanded around-the-world race in 1969, one of the competitors sent his photos by slingshot. He would summon a passing freighter by flag or hand signals, then launch a small container of exposed film with a slingshot, usually with enough accuracy to land the missile on the ship's deck. The same competitor also used his trusty slingshot to communicate, dropping personal letters and reports to race organizers onto passing vessels.

The fellow with the slingshot could have used a more modern form of communication if he had wanted to; the race sponsor, the *Sunday Times* of London, offered him a powerful radio transmitter. He declined, because he loved his slingshot—"A good slingshot is worth all the transmitters in the world," he wrote—and because he was Bernard Moitessier, who always did things a little differently.

Moitessier established his reputation for being different by sailing around the world in that race, then deciding not to finish, because he just didn't want to stop sailing.

Moitessier comes to mind because he is the inspiration for a sailing adventure that has the promise of being even stranger than his own. Reid Stowe plans to sail nonstop for 1,000 days. That would apparently set a record, but that's not the strange part. He plans to do this without ever, once he's cleared shore, seeing land. Moitessier, who died in 1994, would have related to this.

Stowe will sail the self-built 70-foot steel schooner he has lived on and sailed far and wide, including around Cape Horn, for 20 years. His crew will consist of his girlfriend and two cats.

Stowe said the idea for his marathon grew out of a meeting with Moitessier on Tahiti, where Moitessier landed when he finally stopped sailing. Moitessier must have cast quite a spell. Stowe is quoted as saying, "I continually live in a spiritual state at sea," which is pure Moitessier. His book **The Long Way** is full of spirits.

Stowe and his friend will live mainly on nuts, dried oats and sprouts grown on board. He also plans to carry along some bags of dirt. This is meant as a gesture of respect to Mother Earth, but brings to mind a truly awful movie named **Waterworld**, in which scruffy survivors, who are living on boats in a post-nuclear world where no land can be found, revere dirt.

Moitessier carried no soil with him on his husky 40-foot ketch *Joshua*. He did try raising sprouts, but not for long—he threw them overboard in frustration. It seems he wasn't a sprout and nut lover anyway. He carried more than a year's worth of provisions on that first Golden Globe Race (to be prepared for dismasting or shipwreck, he wrote, not in anticipation of beginning a second circumnavigation) including a lot of canned soup and army biscuits, with some goodies, like a nice fat ham, stashed away for special occasions. Though he was born in Vietnam he showed his French lineage in his provisioning. There was ample wine and a bottle of champagne for each of the three capes that had to be rounded in the race, each of which he drained in one sitting and with evident joy.

Those worldly weaknesses aside, Moitessier was well cast as a spiritual sailing guru. He sailed in the company of spirits and frequently communicated with them in their incarnations as dolphins, birds, the sun, wind and sky, and the sea itself. In **The Long Way** it is clear that Moitessier achieved what so many sailors have vainly sought—to be one with the sea. He wrote: "I listen to the sails talking with the rain and the stars amid the sounds of the sea ... the silences full of secret things between my boat and me, like the times I spent as a child listening to the forest talk."

This mystical equilibrium served Moitessier well. On his epic one and a half times around the world race-cruise he endured the savagery of the sea with an equanimity that was almost spooky. It helped, of course, that the lean, muscular Moitessier, he of the flowing, shoulder-length mane and heroic Gallic profile, was a splendid sailor who learned his skills on the Gulf of Siam, where the fishermen who were his mentors prided themselves on navigating without a compass. (Moitessier carried one, but disparaged it as "that god of the west.")

Stowe had better use a compass, not to mention a sextant or, if it's not too much of a concession to this age of high-tech materialism, a GPS, lest he stray and inadvertently see a hump of land on the horizon and sink his dream.

Stowe's is one sailing adventure I don't envy. I have too many spirits on land to stay in touch with. Still, I understand how he fell in the thrall of the man who refused to cross the finish line. You only have to listen to Moitessier: "I am a citizen of the most beautiful nation on earth. A nation whose laws are harsh yet simple, a nation that never cheats, which is immense without borders, where life is lived in the present. In this limitless nation, this nation of wind, light and peace, there is no other ruler besides the sea."

Too Bad the
Clipper Couple Aren't Here
for The Race

THERE is a touching moment in the saga of *Flying Cloud* when the husband and wife who are driving the clipper ship into seafaring history with a record-setting Cape Horn passage realize how fast they are sailing.

The husband and wife are Perkins and Ellen Creesy, he the iron-willed captain, she the bold navigator. *Flying Cloud* has rounded the Horn and is sailing northward well off the coast of Chile in a southeast gale. The dead-aft wind is so strong, the seas so high, that Capt. Creesy, a relentless driver always loath to reduce sail, has ordered the largest sails furled. Even so, the ship, some 8,000 miles into her maiden passage, has never seemed so fast.

When the storm eases and graybeards are no longer sweeping the deck, Perkins and Ellen make their way aft to the taffrail with the log, the clever device that gave sailors the word "knot" as a measure of speed. The log consists of a weighted, wedge-shaped piece of wood attached to a line knotted at 48-foot intervals. When paid out from a moving vessel in an elapsed time of 28 seconds, the knots equal nautical miles traveled in an hour.

The wedge is tossed off the stern, the 28-second sand glass is turned, a crew man feeds the knotted line off of a reel at a furious pace. Perkins and Ellen count the flying knots with a sense of disbelief . . . 10, 15, 16, 17 and finally 18 before the sand has run out.

They look at each other, astonished, in awe of their vessel. In years of sailing mighty ships through the windiest, roughest regions of the oceans, they have never sailed this fast. David W. Shaw, who tells the Creesys' story in the recently published book **Flying Cloud**, imagines that Ellen "delighted in the thrill of the moment and was mindful that no other human beings on earth had ever before experienced such fantastic sailing."

Eighteen knots. Let's see . . . Today a 30-foot sport boat can exceed that in a breezy afternoon buoy race on Long Island Sound. Sailing across the Atlantic last summer, the 110-foot catamaran *Club Med* sailed at an average speed of 26 knots during one 24-hour period. Several of the boats that will start the around-the-world race called The Race will, their designers predict, sail faster than 40 knots.

Sailors in The Race may well experience an epiphany like Ellen Creesy's, the realization that they are sailing at speeds never before experienced under sail on the open ocean. It is quite possible that at least one of the boats in The Race will record a run of more than 700 miles in a day—an *average* speed of 30 knots or more.

These boats are as different from a clipper ships as a sailboat can be, but in one sense they are similar. Like *Flying Cloud*, they are outrageous, radical, risky stabs at heretofore impossible sailing speeds.

How risky? If they are realists, crews on the boats built specifically for The Race know that chances are very good that they will not reach the finish line. The three biggest, fastest boats have already failed in conditions much milder than they will find in the far southern latitudes.

PlayStation, Steve Fossett's 105-foot catamaran, is being lengthened to 125 feet in an attempt to cure a tendency to pitchpole. When the boat nearly flipped end over end in a squall off the coast of England, Fossett said it was one of his scariest experiences. This from a professional daredevil who has ditched in the ocean more than once attempting to circumnavigate the world in hot air balloons.

Grant Dalton, skipper of *Club Med*, one of three sisterships designed by Gilles Ollier for The Race, sent the 110-foot catamaran back to the shop for strengthening after one of its bows collapsed during a New York-to-England run.

Even a christening by Queen Elizabeth herself could not ensure good fortune for Pete Goss' far-out catamaran *Team Philips*. In an ignominious end to its first day of sailing, the boat lost the front 45 feet of one of its hulls. Most radical of the monster cats built for The Race, Goss' boat is 120 feet long, 70 feet wide and features one giant Windsurferlike sail on each on each of the narrow, sharp hulls that are designed to pierce, rather than ride over, waves.

All of which means that things are going about as expected. These designs are supposed to be risky; that's the whole point. There are no rules concerning boat design in The Race. In fact, there are hardly any rules at all, the main one being, first boat around the world gets $1 million (a somewhat disappointing jackpot considering the cost of the boats). Designers and builders have to venture into the unknown to get an edge in this competition. That's how we got to the point where the speed that so amazed Perkins and Ellen Creesy is now routine.

We might temper our self-congratulation, though, by remembering that it has taken us a century and a half to get here. (*Flying Cloud* set the New York to San Francisco sailing record of 89 days, 21 hours in 1851. She set a new record in 1854, which wasn't broken until 1989—by Warren Luhrs in a 60-foot monohull.)

Remember too that *Flying Cloud* sailed at 18 knots, and certainly faster at some moments, going *through* the water, not over it as catamarans do. We're not talking about piercing waves, like Goss' machine might do if it can keep its bows on, but about displacing 1,782 tons of water, not counting hundreds more tons of cargo and stores, a menagerie of livestock, a crew of 65, and 11 passengers.

Donald McKay, *Flying Cloud*'s legendary designer and builder, ventured as much into the unknown as the The Race boat designers, and without computer predictions to guide him. He created *Cloud*'s lines by carving a half hull model. He defied conventional square-rigger wisdom with a fine, concave bow and narrow beam—a mere 41feet on a 235-foot-long hull—then piled on sail, guessing what the boat and rig could take. The three masts of 109, 113 and 127 feet carried 21 sails, not counting the studdingsails that were attached to the ends of the yards for running. The carbon fiber masts of VLMHs (very large multihulls) in The Race are taller, but weigh only a tiny fraction of the clipper ship's spars. The bottom 89-foot section alone of *Cloud*'s three-piece pine mainmast weighed 13 tons.

In hands other than the Creesys' *Flying Cloud* might have been just one of the plethora of clipper ships that flourished for less than a decade before they were made obsolete by steamships. Capt. Creesy was apparently fearless, a hard case little loved by his crew. He drove his ship with small regard for safety, much less comfort. In the gale off the coast of Chile, passengers cowered below as the over-canvassed clipper broached and was overtaken by breaking seas that raked the deck from stern to stem.

Ellen Creesy, the 36-year-old navigator brought so fascinatingly to life in Shaw's book, probably deserves more credit for the speed record than her hard-driving husband. Taught the use of the sextant by her sea captain father, she was a skilled, precise navigator, but it was Ellen's courage in following the then new and controversial routing directions of Matthew Maury that made the difference for *Flying Cloud*, which she took far out of the way to find favorable wind and current.

I'll make no predictions about the outcome of The Race. But I can say this: If Perkins and Ellen Creesy were sailing one of the boats, my money would be on them.

For the Love
of Sailing

The Man
who Loved Sailing

MY father taught me to sail. Then he taught me to love sailing, by his example. I've never met anyone who loved sailing as he did.

I truly believe that for him sailing was a transcendental experience elevated above the level of pastime, hobby, recreation or sport.

I sailed with him boy and man, and witnessed his love of sailing manifested in an abiding appreciation of the harmony of nature with what he believed was one of man's most noble objects, a sailboat. It didn't matter what face nature was wearing at the moment; if he was sailing, it was where he wanted to be. Many were the times when, curled in the cockpit, cold, wet and queasy, I desperately wanted to be anywhere else in the world, while he, at the helm, was content, a man at peace amid the chaos of the storm. Ever the encouraging optimist, he would say above the gale's howl, "Don't worry, it's diminishing, it'll be over soon." Or, "The wind's veering, in a little while we'll be on a comfortable reach." These predictions rarely proved true, but he believed them. He always saw sailing in the most generous light.

He cruised and he raced, not to reach a destination or win a trophy, but just to be there, sailing. He was utterly sound in his sailing knowledge and was a superior helmsman, sensitive to each nuance of the wind and waves and the boat's angle of heel, but he was no great shakes as a racer. I'm sure it was because he refused to commit to the harsh intensity of the competition for fear it would dull his sense of the sailing aesthetics he worshiped.

He read, I believe, most of the words written about sailing, everything from Joshua Slocum to Uffa Fox, and was steeped in its lore, lexicon and principles.

A man of diverse creative gifts, he wrote about sailing, photographed it and painted it. And in 1966 he founded a magazine named *SAILING* to honor its beauty.

As a teenager, he built a sailing dinghy, from scratch. The boats that followed, after college and marriage, were nearly as humble—a used centerboard one-design called a Seagull and an ancient Star.

He sailed as a member of the crew of some of the fast offshore racing boats of the time. His habit of interrupting the sometimes ribald commentary of the crew to wax eloquent over the grandeur of a squall or the glory of a sunrise or the beauty of a certain boat inspired his mates to nickname him The Professor.

He dreamed of owning a new sailboat, beautiful and sleek and big enough to allow him to share what he loved with others, and in 1951 he bought a Dragon class sloop fitted with a cuddy cabin and a couple of berths. Not long ago I came across the invoice in a file of some of his sailing papers: "One Dragon Class racing cruising deluxe model, 29'2" sloop, complete with sails, equipment, rigging, loose items and all finishing—$4,560."

The boat was imported from Norway, complete with a Norwegian, who came to rig it, but spent most of his time trying to keep it afloat. Built of African mahogany and finished bright, it was as impressive an example of the woodworker's craft as the most exquisite piece of furniture. Better it had been treated as furniture and never been launched. It was a chronic leaker. Worn down by dealing with the near sinking that each spring's launch brought, my father sold the boat after a few seasons, jaded about boat ownership, though no less in love with sailing.

It wasn't until the fiberglass era arrived, bringing with it the promise of boats that would never leak, that he bought another sailboat, a yawl designed by his favorite designer, Phil Rhodes, that could accommodate all of our large family. There were idyllic moments on that boat, sunny times of gentle wind and calm water when it was easy to love sailing, and times when it wasn't so easy. No one who was aboard will forget when, at the start of a family cruise, a sunset dinner was blown away by a sudden arrival of a cold front, a prelude to a hard night's passage through a gale that blew out sails, caused seasickness and general misery and made the boat's interior look as though it had been bombed. I remember looking aft in the black night and seeing my father in his place at the helm in front of a dramatic background of cresting seas. He wore that small smile that said he was exactly where he wanted to be. Then, as I had come to expect, he said, "It's calming down, we'll be sailing more comfortably soon."

I think of these things from the perspective of *SAILING*'s 30th anniversary. He died when the magazine was in its infancy, leaving me and another sailor who was fortunate enough to be influenced by his love of sailing, my sister Micca Hutchins, and a band of gifted journalists and lovers of sailing he never met, as stewards of his dream of celebrating the love of sailing in words and pictures.

How would he, the man who loved sailing, feel about *SAILING* if he could see it today? I'm proud to say … he would love it.

Sailing is About Taking the Time

AT a meeting of a sailing trade organization, I learned that, according to a new survey, the average American sailboat owner uses his or her boat a mere 56 hours a year.

That brought to mind a friend who meticulously records, to the nearest quarter hour, the time he spends on his boat. At the end of the season he divides that number into the amount of money he spent on the boat that year to derive an hourly cost for his sailing enjoyment. He says the result is always distressing but has a bright side in that it motivates him to use his boat more.

I've long thought my friend might be happier tying flies or building model airplanes or pursuing some other cheap, time-intensive hobby that would make his math look better.

For my part, I don't need any extra motivation to go sailing. And I certainly am not interested in punishing myself by analyzing the cost of my fun. But I am concerned about taking the time to go sailing. It seems to be getting harder to do that, and that's distressing. Because sailing is about taking the time.

It was mentioned at that industry gathering—by sailing television commentator Gary Jobson, no less—that trends are evident that support the idea that sailing time is getting shorter. Weekend getaways are replacing extended cruises. Distance racing is in decline. Regattas that cram lots of short races into two or three days of frenetic sailing and party activity are the rage.

Nothing wrong with any of that. (In fact, those condensed, action-packed regattas are making sailboat racing more enjoyable, especially for wives and children who prefer not be abandoned, as often happened when dad disappeared over the horizon for days with his buddies on a distance race.) But it begs the question of what happened to our time.

Fewer people are taking the water rat's advice about messing about in boats. *Carpe diem* is still a popular boat name, but with the average sailboat owner seizing only four and a half days a year for sailing, we're apparently not taking the mother of all life-affirming mottos seriously.

Too bad, because this is no time to be stinting on sailing time. Sailing is the antidote to the excessive busy-ness that consumes us.

Sailing takes time, and it gives us the time to experience nuances of pleasure rarely found elsewhere. The satisfying rhythm of a boat under sail on a rolling sea. The company of kindred spirits in the awe-inspiring amphitheater of sky and sea. The reward, at the end of the watch, of a warm berth and the serenade of the sea rushing by the hull. The purity of the wilderness we find a few hours offshore. The independence. The self-reliance.

I'm preaching it, but I've been poor at practicing it of late. What passes for a cruise nowadays for me and my sailing companion is a long delivery home from a long-distance race. It's supposed to be a leisurely affair, but there always seems to be a schedule, never the luxury of dawdling.

It wasn't like that when we had our first cruising boat. I still don't quite understand how we managed it. We had a struggling business to worry about, little children to place with grandparents, mortgage payments to make. Yet we took the time for a summer cruise. It wasn't a lot of time, but we spent it as though it would never end.

On the second morning of that cruise we awoke to the tapping of halyard against the mast, a welcome signal of the arrival of a breeze from the northeast, not strong, but steady and dependable out of a benign, slow-moving high. It came from the direction we wanted to sail. Today, I would be all too inclined to set the mainsail, start the engine and motorsail to the next port. But then, in those innocent days before we were important enough to feel we had to keep schedules even while sailing, we regarded the morning breeze as a gift that would be a sin to squander. We raised the sails, sheeted in and … just sailed.

Through the day we sailed, full and by, on long tacks that took us so far out that the shore was just a gray squiggle on the horizon, and then back near enough to the beach to hear the bark of a dog over the muted fall of the surf. The atmosphere, unsullied by stain of pollution or even a vagrant cloud, magnified the searing sun. But the cool wind and the hot sun took the edge off each other, and the cockpit of our little boat was an island of perfect temperate weather. In swimming suits, we trimmed a sail when we felt like it, steered by the feel of the wind in our faces with only occasional reference to telltale or compass, read books, had lunch, talked on and on, all to the accompaniment of the burbling bow wave. We sailed the day away on a sea corduroyed by small waves too gentle to curl into whitecaps, and felt like privileged intruders in a pristine blue world.

Our boat was only a 30-footer. The wind could have been blowing no more than 8 or 9 knots. Our VMG toward our intended destination was probably around 3 knots. It was a slow way to get anywhere. And we could not have cared less. How could getting there be better than this?

At that trade meeting some ideas were offered on how to persuade time-crunched Americans to take up sailing. I'm sure they are good ideas, but I have a better one. If we could capture the magic of that day so long ago when we just took the time to enjoy sailing and include a bottle of it with every boat, you couldn't build them fast enough.

875 Miles to Bermuda in Winter: It was Just a Test

THOUGH we had interrupted their ongoing midwinter afternoon card game, the three customs officers who stepped aboard, still buttoning uniforms and arranging hats, were delighted to see us. Manning the customs office on the quay at St. George's, Bermuda, in February is a lonely job. The winter personality of the North Atlantic has a way of discouraging visitors to what Bermudians proudly claim to be the second most isolated inhabited island in the world.

And so the first question the customs men asked of the four unshaven, red-eyed sailors in salt encrusted foul weather gear was: What on earth made you sail to Bermuda this time of year?

Well, we were testing a sailboat.

You've seen those television commercials in which robotic devices test an automobile—slamming doors a couple of million times, driving into brick walls and otherwise abusing it—to show how tough it is. Warren Luhrs decided to do something like that to a boat. Instead of robots, four humans would conduct the test. The laboratory would be the Atlantic Ocean. In February.

The idea was to sail a new Passage 42 built by Hunter Marine—Luhrs' company—from St. Augustine, Florida, to Bermuda to see whether the boat achieves its design goal of being both a plushly decorated, center cockpit, live-aboard yacht and an able offshore passagemaker.

The test crew consisted of:

Luhrs. Besides running sailboat and powerboat building companies, he dabbles in sailing adventure. A veteran of the OSTAR and BOC singlehanded challenges, he is preparing an exotic new greyhound of a sailboat, the 60-foot *Hunter's Child*, for the BOC singlehanded around-the-world race. His place in sailing history is assured: Last spring he became the first sailor to break the New York to San Francisco passage record, held for 185 years by the clippership *Flying Cloud*.

Lars Bergstrom. Swedish inventer, designer, philosopher and world class optimist, Bergstrom has sailed far and wide, including around the Horn with best buddy Luhrs on the record breaking run.

Paul Sandberg. A sailing professional currently working on the *Hunter's Child* project, Sandberg has sailed more than 100,000 miles.

Me.

How did the test go? Let me summarize our findings: There's a good reason the Bermuda customs office has little business in winter. The term accurate weather forecast is not an oxymoron. Seasickness remains a great social leveler. The boat acquitted itself well, though modifications to the sunbathing deck are indicated.

Bob Rice, the sailors' weather guru of Bedford, Massachusetts, looked a week into the future and told us, with uncanny accuracy, what the weather on the Atlantic Ocean would be. He said it would be windy and unsettled, with winds up to 45 knots, rain squalls, cloudy skies with a few sunny periods, a generally clocking breeze, and it was all of that. Only the east wind Rice forecast for our final day of sailing failed to materialize, which made it a fair wind voyage, 875 nautical miles reaching and running from St. Augustine to Gibb's Hill light on the southwest tip of Bermuda.

We spent five days and two hours getting to Bermuda in a breeze so consistently strong (except for a rainy morning spent powering) that main and genoa were always reefed and, except for time spent below, we were always in foul weather gear. By noon of our first day the south wind had breezed up to a whistling 30 knots with steep whitecapped seas. After dark, squalls sneaked up, invisible in the moonless, starless night but announced by the chill vapors that preceded them, intruding into the Gulfstream-warmed air. The squalls piled rain, screeching gusts and chaotic seas on the already boisterous Atlantic.

As we bashed our way along the rhumbline, guided by loran which didn't lose its signal until we had seen Gibb's Hill light, the wind clocked slowly from south to north, giving us several days of high intensity downwind sailing. With the genoa furled and the mainsail reefed to the maximum, the husky 42 barreled down the long, bumpy waves like a fearless skier on a mogul-studded slope. In the cockpit, our heavy clothing plastered to our backsides by the powerful westerly, we saw 12-knot bursts on the boat speed meter and a gust of 50 knots on the wind meter—that was 50 apparent, dead downwind.

Looking astern from the helm, the seas sometimes filled the sky, and I was reminded of words from an old patriotic song, "purple mountains' majesty." In the sun the great, dark waves turned vivid purple—purple mountains topped with snowy white where the wind has stirred up galloping white horses with manes that would blow away in trails of spume.

This was a lonely ocean that we shared only with some vagrants of the sea—brown tufts of sargasso weed and fleets of Portuguese men-o-war that looked like inflatable toy boats—a few dolphins and flying fish.

The boat's motion on the constantly riled ocean was, well, challenging. Early on it established the fact that not even a seasickness-free Cape Horn passage is a guarantee that old devil *mal de mer* won't pay a visit. It got us all sooner or later, even Lars, who in his mid-50s experienced seasickness for the first time in his life. Typically, he did it with a smile.

Winds of more than 50 knots, high seas, nasty squalls, seasickness ... a perilous voyage, fraught with misery and worry? On the contrary, this was a happy, laid-back, no-sweat passage, marked by not so much as a raised voice or even a minor emergency. We stood watches in pairs and never once felt the need to call our sleeping offwatch mates on deck early. Covered to the eyes against the incessant spray (with plenty of layers during the cool days after we crossed the main flow of the Gulfstream), we hooked safety harnesses onto the handy stainless steel radar arch over the cockpit and served our four hours (speaking for myself, at least) marveling at the Atlantic theater and dreaming of the warm berth that awaited below. At odd moments, lest anyone take things too seriously, Lars would pop out of the companionway, duck a wave, comment on what a lovely day it was and record the scene with his splashproof camcorder.

The crew passed the test, but what about the boat? The Passage 42 took it all in stride, proving herself a fast off-the-wind sailer (averaging more than seven knots on a 36-foot waterline) strong of hull and rig and, despite all the spray and solid water coming aboard, cozy and dry below. Our most serious equipment problem was the loss of the cushions from the sunbathing platform atop the aft cabin, which carried away in squall. A great tan was not a priority anyway.

At the dock in the all but deserted harbor of St. George's, our yacht's saloon, with its big oval table and thick, soft seats, appeared so comfortable and organized that a customs agent remarked that it hardly looked as though we had made the crossing from the U.S.A.

I suspect he thought it was all a joke, that we had just motored in from Hamilton, Bermuda's other harbor.

Lives Enriched by
Voyaging Under Sail

MY second-favorite sailing magazine is really a newsletter, the Cruising Club of America's.

Its arrival invariably brings a pleasant twinge of nostalgia. Its uncoated paper and newspaper web press printing remind me of *SAILING* in the early years before it was glossy and full of color.

The reason I love reading the CCA News, though, is that it is a chronicle of the sailing experiences of a group of people who have enriched their lives remarkably by voyaging under sail.

The stories of these CCA members make fascinating reading in spite of their authors' tendency toward understatement. The Atlantic crossing or the long run down the Pacific are treated as routine. Passages to distant and exotic or even dangerous landfalls are written of, not as great adventures or particularly noteworthy accomplishments, but as joyous experiences that bring together the satisfactions of sailing, intimacy with the ocean environment and the company of good friends.

Some of these stories are told in the obituaries, which are long and detailed, as they must be to summarize lives so crowded with incident, adventure and achievement as those of so many CCA members. Business or military accomplishments are noted amid more lengthy reporting on the fascinating items of lives nurtured by sailing—boats owned, ocean races won, cruising passages made.

Hearing of such things firsthand, from CCA members who are very much alive, was one of the pleasures of being at the Blue Water Weekend at Annapolis, which marked the club's 75th anniversary. Another was the opportunity to meet or renew acquaintances with winners of the Blue Water Medal, which has been awarded by the CCA for "meritorious examples of seamanship" since 1923.

The medalists have recorded great adventures, but most of them would not want to be called adventurers. They are amateur sailors, a requirement for the Blue Water award. Their feats, with few exceptions, did not put their names in record books. They sailed for the richness of the experience rather than public acclaim. Eighteen of them were at the CCA gathering. Let me introduce you to a few of them:

Jacqueline and Christiane Darde are petite French sisters. They spent six years sailing a 30-foot sloop around the world. Then they set off again, this time on a seven-year voyage in a 38-foot boat. In awarding the medal in 1994, the CCA noted, in language that could well describe the approach many of its own members take to ocean cruising, that the Darde sisters faced the challenges of their long voyages "with competence, grace and humor."

Tim Carr came to the Blue Water Weekend from South Georgia Island, which halved the population of the tiny island that sits in the Southern Ocean 2,500 miles due east of Cape Horn. Tim and his wife Pauline are its only residents. Their medal, given in 1991, recognizes 23 years of world cruising in *Curlew*, a 28-foot Falmouth Quay punt built in 1898. The gaff-rigged boat has no engine, no electronics of any kind. On receiving the award, Pauline spoke words that sounded like an environmentalist's poem: "It is better to leave no tracks, no signs of man's passing, and our wake soon melts back into the waves."

Hal and Margaret Roth, between them, have sailed more than

a quarter million miles. They received the Blue Water Medal in 1971 for sailing 18,538 of those miles in a voyage around the Pacific basin that went as far as Japan, the Aleutians and Alaska along a route never before taken by a cruising sailboat.

Their cruises have been as much cultural explorations as sailing passages. They've called at remote islands and poked into out-of-the-way ports, taking the time to become familiar with all that is indigenous, especially the people. Their wanderings over the years have left in their wake a collection of people of various nationalities who befriended the man and woman who sailed into their lives on a 35-foot sailboat named *Whisper*.

The Roths are known to thousands more through Hal's numerous books, including **Two on a Big Ocean**, the story of their first Pacific cruise. The cruising and the resulting books have been their life's work ever since the 1960s, when they took a sailing lesson, bought a boat and sailed away (with interruptions when Hal took off to sail in two BOC solo around-the-world races). Now, at a time in their lives when others their age are nestled in secure retirement, the Roths are carrying on business as usual—going sailing. This time it is a cruise along the course Odysseus sailed in Homer's epic poem, which will yield Hal's next book. The current, and final, leg starts from Malta. When they've finished it, Hal and Margaret will again be two on a big ocean as they sail their 35-foot Pretorian sloop across the Atlantic to a berth near their land home on St. Michaels on the Eastern Shore of Maryland.

On the wall of that home is a splendid photograph taken by Hal that speaks volumes about the way the dauntless sailors who have won the Blue Water Medal, and, for that matter, the cheerful cruisers of the CCA, go about their sailing. It was taken off the coast of Tierra del Fuego in the neighborhood of Cape Horn, a nasty neighborhood indeed at the time of the photo. The enormous seas, tops blown off by a gale, are veined with foam. Snow is drifted on the cabintop of *Whisper*, which is running under bare pole. Margaret, sleet melting on her face under her oilskin hood, is steering.

She is smiling.

Sailing with Kids
Improves with Age

THIS summer, on a fine looking red boat, Erin will sail her first Chicago-Mackinac Race.

Erin is 16, and she is my daughter. Her presence on the rail or in the cockpit (though not, perish the thought, in the galley) in this race that is the centerpiece of our sailing season will be significant in that it will signal her final victory over the disadvantages of a childhood of sailing.

Her brother Bill, who is 20 and has sailed a number of Mackinac races, experienced a similar rite of passage as a teenager.

To my profound relief, it now seems we—my wife Jean and I—did no permanent damage by acting like a parental press gang and dragging these children to sea at tender ages.

They both sailed before they walked. I can still see Bill in one of those seats that are suspended in a sort of circular roll bar affair on wheels that pre-toddlers sit in to experience their first adventure in ambulation. Children brought up normally do that in their homes. Our son was in the cockpit of a sailboat. Fortunately, it was a narrow cockpit, so he rolled only forward and aft with the motion of the boat between the steering pedestal and the bridgedeck.

Sailing with children has been the subject of innumerable articles in sailing magazines, even entire books. Children don't write these, of course, so the viewpoint is adult. We are told sailing with the kids is an ennobling experience, and it frequently is—for the parents. Doing things as a family radiates all sorts of good feelings for parents, to say nothing of cutting babysitting costs.

Now, try to imagine family sailing from the kids' perspective. You're taken out of a comfortable home, away from your favorite toys, away from TV, made to wear bulky life preservers and confining safety harnesses in a claustrophobic, wet, cold and constantly moving environment. Social workers have called nicer experiences child abuse.

It is mostly the motion that makes sailing hell for young children. Children get seasick. There is no escape, except to sail only on calm water. On a long spring cruise on Lake Superior in pre-Transderm Scop days, six-year-old Erin spent the sailing hours of seven straight days wedged in a pilot berth with a Barbie Doll and a bucket, snoozing, playing, munching the occasional soda cracker and throwing up. What do you suppose she was thinking when her parents got all dewy-eyed at cocktail hour over the joys of sailing?

Still, I hope she and her brother have some happy memories of those early sailing days. Certainly, I do.

Times ashore in cruising ports were some of the best times, not surprising considering how desperate the children were to get off the boat. While I spent those sun-drenched days in the exquisite pursuit of what Kenneth Grahame's water rat called "simply messing around in boats"—cleaning, taping, splicing and doing other unnecessary tasks—the children explored places that must have seemed exotic. They swam, and angled for hours on end for the perch and bass they were certain were lurking beneath the docks. On one such day at a primitive island pier, Jean was startled by a vaguely familiar form descending rapidly past the galley window. When it dawned on her that it was her firstborn falling into the drink, she rushed topside and had him out in a jiffy. Mothers are known to have superhuman strength in such situations, but this quick rescue was probably more attributable to the fact that little Bill had seen some large water snakes in the vicinity, the memory of which contributed to a panic induced act of levitation.

Still vivid in my memory are images from a magical night in the Upper Michigan ghost town of Fayette. With the boat snug in Snailshell Harbor below, we played hide and seek among the spooky century-old buildings in the eerie orange light of an electrical storm approaching over the bay. We all saw ghosts that night.

There are racing memories too, though they come with twinges of guilt. There was the time Erin's babysitter wasn't available for a race one breezy autumn afternoon. I cajoled: The wind is offshore; it will be calm; you'll see, it will be fun. Erin agreed to sail, and, of course, the wind changed; the seas rose; the race was a fire drill from start to finish. The poor kid not only got sick, but when she retreated below she was buried under a wet spinnaker and then walked on by an unknowing crewmember. Back in the marina, a soaked, shivering, bruised, very angry young lady jumped onto the dock, put her hands on her hips, turned to her father and snarled: "You call that fun?"

And the time that a very young Bill was in the cockpit when our 40-footer spun into a long, shuddering broach. With the boat on her beam-ends my first instinct was to keep the lad, then prone in the cockpit, aboard the boat. So I put my foot on him while I shouted useless instructions at the crew. This worked fine until the cockpit started to fill. Bill finally made enough of a fuss to get me to remove my foot, and he bobbed to the surface of cockpit/bathtub, unhurt but extremely irritated.

And now these kids love to race. Amazing.

This is a bittersweet time. Those family cruises I remember so fondly are, I fear, things of the past. The lives of this soon-to-be college junior and high school junior are too busy to have time for going places just for the fun of it at six knots. Yet they love sailing so much that they are even willing to do it with their parents. (They apparently don't care, or are unaware, that we are blowing their inheritance on boats.)

I am more than relieved that my son and daughter enjoy sailing in spite of having been forced as children to serve before the mast; I am delighted to have them in the crew, to have Bill prowling the foredeck with his sailing savvy and muscles, to have Erin aboard with her fierce streak of competitiveness (this girl doesn't just want to beat the other boats—she wants to sink them). These two are good sailors. They should be—they've been sailing all their lives.

I guess I'm just lucky. I didn't plan it this way. Honest.

Tonic for the Human Spirit

I love sailing best when it gets a little difficult.

Sailing is an easy, safe thing to do. But you can always find a challenge in it if that's what you want—to make a competent passage in boisterous weather, to race well against good sailors in good boats, to bring the boat smartly to the dock under sail. In times so obsessed with security—times so fearful, some might say—that wine bottles come with warning labels, sailing still offers a tantalizing taste of risk. For most of us, it is tiny risk, maybe just the risk of embarrassment, maybe just a Walter Mitty risk. Still, this is the mystique of sailing, the atavistic pull of challenging the splendid, sometimes daunting forces of nature, even if mostly in our dreams.

No wonder, then, that we are fascinated by the dangerous quests of this age's sailing adventurers, the men and women who sail radically designed sailboats, often alone, through the most treacherous reaches of the oceans in pursuit of celebrity and wealth and, in some cases, the chance to make sailing history by doing what has never been done before.

Some of us, that is, are fascinated. Others are irritated, or worse, judging from some of the letters I received following the loss at sea of Mike Plant, America's best known adventure sailor. Several of the letters scolded me for failing to point out the dangers of sailing boats such as Plant's and even posthumously scolded Plant for pushing the limits of safety at sea.

Call me naive, but I thought everyone knew that Plant's boat and all the others like it sailing the oceans today are dangerous and that the kind of sailing he did and scores of other adventurers are doing is hazardous to their health. I didn't know we were supposed to attach a "Don't try this at home" warning label to our stories about them.

Anyone who thinks these sailors are on this earth to be exemplars of the principles of safe sailing missed the point a long time ago. They live in the world of the test pilot, Indy car driver and mountain climber. Safety, to the degree that we insist on it for our own purely-for-enjoyment sailing, has small place in this world. Mike Plant would have been safe in a sturdy Valiant 47, and probably miserable because he would have had no chance of winning the Globe Challenge. He lost his life in a boat that could have won the race, a boat in which much of what we equate with safety was exchanged for the speed that is a requisite for the successes Mike Plant sought with such a passion.

If Plant's 60-foot monohull *Coyote* was, as one reader put it in a letter, "on the edge," some of the boats now trying to win the Jules Verne Trophy by sailing around the world in 80 days— they'll have to *average* about 14 knots—have gone beyond the edge. Consider, for example, an 85-foot catamaran: crewmen, who when off watch live in capsule-like spaces in four-foot wide hulls, work clinging to a 40-foot long between-hull stringer as though it were a yardarm on a clipper ship while their space age wind craft streaks over waves at 30 knots.

Critics who suggested that Mike Plant in his risky transatlantic dash in an untested boat somehow betrayed the ethic of seamanship perhaps think of these sailing adventurers as daredevils, stunt drivers on water, mercenaries who devalue life in pursuit of glory and the paychecks that will follow. I think of them as great sailors. I'm proud to have them a part—albeit an exotic, out-of-the-mainstream part—of our sport. We've used up a lot of our world's possibilities; it's a tonic for the human spirit to know that there are some left, new frontiers for the boldest sailors, combining high-tech, old-fashioned bravery and, yes, seamanship of the highest order, to cross.

What, then, of the argument that the public shouldn't have to pay for rescuing adventurers who willingly put themselves in harm's way? *Yachting* magazine's spin on that notion was to point out that the considerable sum of money spent searching for Plant would have paid for vaccinations for lots of children.

Interesting thought. And if the owners of the so-called superyachts catered to by *Yachting* would contribute, say, two percent of their annual fuel expense to a vaccination fund, even more kids could get shots.

Deciding who qualifies for rescue—maybe whose life will be saved—sounds a lot like playing God. Even so, it probably wouldn't make much difference to the record-chasing sailors if they had to sign off on rescue at public expense. If they were worried about being rescued they'd be in a different line of work.

Surprisingly few of them ever need rescuing anyway. For those who do in waters served by the U.S. Coast Guard, I'm happy to contribute a few tax dollars to keep these daring men and women around. This would surely be a diminished planet without them.

Schooner Sailing in the Exumas

MENTION chartering and most of us these days think first of being captain for a week or two of a trim fiberglass sloop island-hopping on turquoise water. Bareboat chartering—a sort of Everyman's key to paradise—has turned sailing fantasies into cherished experiences for thousands of sailors. My own highlight film of sailing experiences is replete with exhilarating passages and exotic landfalls made on sail-it-yourself cruises. Those experiences were enhanced by the satisfying feeling of being in charge of the boat, free from the subtle pressures of having a captain and crew used to doing things their way. Not that there's anything wrong with a crewed charter. In fact, my first—and most sharply remembered—charter was one on which a captain and "crew" were very much in charge.

I put "crew" in quotes because the word doesn't fit Harriet Weeks, who might better have been called the vice-captain. She was the wife of John Weeks, captain of the schooner *Heron*. John, descended from New England sea captains, looked like a character out of Melville with his luxuriant whaler's beard. Striking in her own right, Harriet was tanned to a burnt sienna hue and wore her thick gray hair long. She was a nurse by profession, a cook of gourmet stature, an entertaining raconteur over rum drinks and a formidable second-in-command. Together they owned the old schooner, which I believe represented the sum of their wealth. They made their living chartering in the Bahama out islands.

The term "crewed charter" inspires visions of gleaming bright-
work, bleached teak decks, liveried crew and the other accouter-
ments of a gold-plater. *Heron*, lying at the end of a pier in Yacht
Haven in Nassau harbor, was no gold-plater. She showed her
years and her miles, but the sweet lines of her hull were as true
as when John Alden drew them. I thought she was utterly beautiful.

Jean and I, recently married, were guests of my parents on this
jaunt through the Exumas. The feeling on board, though, was
more that we were guests of the owners, invited to share their
sailing home. With the six of us, plus the hired crewman Shelton,
an island teenager, on board, *Heron* sailed off on a smart reach,
bound for Highbourne Cay.

Heron was a joy. She surged over the startlingly shallow banks
with a muscular grace to the tune of the creaking and squeaking
of wooden blocks and manila line.

For his part, John Weeks was a consummate seaman, patient,
infinitely skilled, perfectly in tune with his boat. At afternoon
landfalls, his execution of the Bahamian moor—precisely placing
two anchors so that the boat would not change position or drag
when the tidal current changed direction—was a ballet in slow
motion. The setting of the two heavy Herreshoff Yachtsman
anchors was never done in less than an hour, and never declared
accomplished until Weeks had inspected the placement of each
anchor from the dinghy, which he invariably referred to as the
"dinghy-boat."

In Waderick Wells, Weeks's mastery of the Bahamian moor
allowed him to tuck the bulky *Heron* in a tidal stream between
the beach and a sandspit that could not have been more than 50
yards apart.

Shelton worked with a will for the captain, who never raised his voice, unlike Harriet, who was wont to aim a withering verbal barrage at the lad. (Even a paying guest could feel the lash of Harriet's tongue for an offense such as stepping aboard with sandy feet.)

Poor Shelton. His worst run-in with Harriet resulted from an incident in which he was the innocent victim. At Staniel Cay, the owners stayed on board while Shelton took us ashore on a mission to find the legendary sailing skipper Rolly Gray. We found him in a rum shop on the side of a hill. While a pair of guitar players and a drummer dressed in zoot suits straight out of *Mad* magazine made godawful noises, we drank rum with Gray and his mates longer than we should have.

On the return trip, Shelton, who had stayed sober as a preacher, had what might charitably be called an unstable load in the dinghy and, of course, we capsized. It was 2 a.m., the anchorage was deserted except for the distant *Heron* and a couple of other yachts, and a strong tidal current was insistently pushing the overturned boat and its five hangers-on offshore.

Shelton, no doubt previewing Harriet's wrath in his mind, tried to put the best face on the situation. "Don't worry, mon," he said, "the tide is slack." (He pronounced it "slaaack.") After I disagreed, pointing out that at the rate we were drifting we would be in the Tongue of the Ocean by sunrise, with Cuba the next stop, the girls did the sensible thing and started hollering their heads off. This eventually woke a friendly yachtsman, who appeared with a dinghy to tow the whole soaked outfit back to *Heron*.

Shelton spent the remainder of the cruise in the doghouse. The rest of us fell easily back into the seductive rhythms of schooner sailing, and finished the cruise on a high note by bounding home to Nassau rail down on Exuma Sound in a fresh westerly.

I've never had a charter like it since. I don't think they make them like that anymore.

A Wry Look
at Sailing

The Lost Art of Broaching

I don't mean to brag, but I have to say we were some of the best broachers around. We could broach faster, more spectacularly, more violently and, certainly, more often than almost any boat we raced against. We could round up and round down. We could bury the spinnaker pole or the boom in the drink with equal ability. Sometimes we buried them both in the same broach—the rare and tricky double compound spin-out in which the boat broaches through a full 360-degree circle. (Although terrifying, this had the advantage of pointing the boat in the right direction once recovery was effected.) I'm proud to say that through all of that broaching we never lost a person overboard or had a crew injury more serious than the occasional mild case of whiplash suffered by crewmembers at the bow or stern where G-forces were greatest during our speed-of-light spin-outs. This was a well-drilled crew, one of the few that actually practiced broaching the way other crews practiced tacking, gybing and changing sails. Unlike those maneuvers, broaching was done without command. It happened too fast for anyone to say, "Ready, broach!"

Though the crew performed admirably, credit for the record of broaching achievement we established in the early and mid-1980s has to go to the boat. It was an IOR design. The initials meant International Offshore Rule, but what they really stood for was Broaching Machine. The refining and inbreeding of design encouraged by that rule led to hulls that were fat in the middle and pinched in the ends. Under the tortured logic of the rule, this yielded a favorable rating. It also made carrying a spinnaker in more than 20 knots of wind a white-knuckle adventure.

My IOR boat is long gone. Its successor, an IMS design, is so stable that we haven't had to use our broaching skills for years. I thought of the old Broaching Machine the other day, though, when I read Roger Marshall's opinion that the IMS, which was supposed to be the antidote to the IOR, is succumbing to the same sort of pressures that gave us squirrely IOR boats and is producing boats that are too light to sail offshore in heavy weather.

When I asked him about this, Marshall, a yacht designer and sailor who has served a lot of time before the mast in rough weather in Bermuda and Fastnet Races, said, "Frankly, I would not want to be out there being pounded for eight or 10 hours or more in these boats in a storm. I don't have confidence in the way they're being built."

Greg Stewart, of Nelson/Marek Yacht Designs, on the other hand, has plenty of confidence. He designs the kind of boats Marshall is talking about and calls them "very wholesome" offshore boats that are "the most stable boats afloat." The latter assertion is backed up by the stability and righting moment numbers on IMS certificates.

One thing the two agree on is that the newest IMS designs put a premium on the builder's art. To turn out a 40-footer weighing 10,000 pounds, of which more than 6,000 pounds is a deep, skinny keel, that can hold together in rough going is a daunting challenge to high-tech construction techniques.

IMS design should be of more than passing interest to sailors who will never enter an IMS race. Cruising design follows racing design. For years, buyers of production built cruiser-racers were sailing IOR hulls. Now the pure, bump-free designs of IMS hulls

translate beautifully to cruising boats that, even with full accommodations and broader, shallower keels, sail with speed and control. They probably represent what the inventors of the IMS had
in mind in the first place.

I can give first-hand testimony to the speed with which the
IMS abandoned its founding ideal of encouraging dual-purpose
boats. My boat is a first-generation IMS design, six years old. It
has nice accommodations. It ought to—it weighs more than twice
as much as comparable new IMS boats.

We have this little joke. When we see the fastest boat in our
fleet, a 1995 IMS design, sail by, we point out that the entire boat
weighs less than our keel alone.

It isn't all that funny, because while we part the seas with a
great show of power amid cascades of green water, the new boat
skips over the waves and sails effortlessly away. Unless fate inter-
venes, as it did one breezy day last fall.

On a downwind leg, the bantamweight suddenly did what
IMS boats aren't supposed to do. It dove into a five-alarm,
Technicolor, monster broach that seemed to last forever. As we
sailed stolidly past some minutes later, enjoying a pleasant rush
of déja vù, the spinnaker was still kissing the water and sheets,
guys and crew were still draped over the lifelines. I can't imagine
how this state-of-the-art IMS boat managed to do a classic IOR
wipeout, but I can hardly fault the crew for taking a long time
getting out of it. These days, you just don't get much opportunity to practice the fine art of broaching.

Sail on It, Drink It

IT'S as dependable as the sunrise. We run out of water in the Chicago-Mackinac Race.

I have been accused of planning this. As evidence, certain crewmembers point out that the taps always run dry at about the same point in the race. One says she knows it's Sunday if she's brushing her teeth with Coke. The navigator is wont to express the boat's position as something like, "Three point five nautical miles southeast of the place where we run out of water." That would be around the middle of the lake, somewhere between the last glimpse of shore, which was of a looming city skyline, and the next, which will be of dunes and trees. This is the point where, in the wisdom of the skipper, the lake water becomes clean enough to drink.

I defend myself against the grousers by observing that they are lucky to have any water at all in the tanks. I point out that the crews of the featherweight Farr and Nelson/Marek boats we race against probably have to subsist on a shared liter of Evian. Since our boat weighs as much as two and a half of these new IMS racers that flaunt their incredible lightness of being by sailing away from us with demoralizing speed, we can afford the weight of a bit of water in the tanks. On the other hand, if it happens to run out at around the place where nature is ready to supply potable water, well, what a happy coincidence.

The legendary purity of the water in the upper reaches of Lake

Michigan is, I will admit, more a matter of lore than of scientific proof. It certainly looks pure. This is lovely water, limpid and cool, embraced by a shore that doesn't look much different than when the French explorers set the first white eyes on it. So, in the thrall of what he believes to be the most beautiful sailing water in the world, the skipper says—Drink heartily, mates.

I read an article that warns that this water is not as pure as it looks. It may harbor contaminants that come not from that forested shore but from the air. This is disillusioning, for the air here is as lovely as the water, so clear that objects, from stars to lighthouses, stand out in startling relief, bigger than life, as though the atmosphere were a magnifying glass.

This seemingly perfect air, we learn in the article, likely transports poisons from far away to be dropped into the seemingly perfect water. Hard to believe as we run down the Straits of Mackinac close to the northern border of the United States that the water below contains DDT from Latin America.

We install holding tanks in our boats, recycle our beer cans and follow complex government rules to protect the environment. Meanwhile the water in one of our pristine places is polluted by a pesticide that has been banned here for years, sent by a third world country—a reminder that it's the global environment that counts and that caring for it is mainly a phenomenon of well-to-do nations. Countries struggling to develop their economies rarely make the cleanliness of the air and water a priority.

The same thought occurred to me while sailing this spring in the Grenadines, where the shimmering clarity of the water inspires awe even though you can't drink it. Here in the lower Windwards, the part of the Caribbean least touched by development, they are building a 300-boat marina at the south end of Union Island. The first rude intrusions of the bulldozers and earth movers are evident in the causeway that now connects

Union with Frigate Island and forms the marina basin that will provide slips for all those boats.

The business people of Union Island are ecstatic at the prospect of the money that will flow into the island economy when the marina opens in a few years, as are development officials of the country of St. Vincent, which is helping to fund the project. But as a visitor from a country that has the luxury of being environmentally correct, I am saddened. The ocean, it's true, is forgiving. Its tides and currents will probably keep what goes into the water at the marina from getting to the glorious reefs of the nearby Tobago Cays. But the concentrated effluent from heads and the toxic leachings from bottom paints will have to go somewhere in this water that looks as though it flowed from paradise.

The Great Lakes don't have cleansing tides. What goes into them tends to stay for a long time. Which is why it probably isn't a good idea to drink the water untreated. Still, I'm going to do it. Not to save the weight of water in the tanks. But to indulge the fond conceit that, where I come from, you can drink the water you sail on.

What the Curse
Tells Us About Sailing

DOCKSIDE in the early morning, after most of the boats had finished, there was a lot of talk about "furlin' and hurlin'." The overnight race had been a fast one with plenty of breeze of the reaching variety, but the sea had been lumpy with steep, confused waves. Old Devil Seasickness rode along on a good many of the boats.

I was pleased that my crew held up well. Even the two who spent a long time in nasty conditions below packing a heavy, sodden 1.5 ounce spinnaker returned to their places on the rail feeling fine. Still, the rough night made me think of D-Day.

Not that I was there for the invasion. I was there, though—in front of a stack of newspapers and magazines and the television—for the saturation coverage of the 50th anniversary of D-Day in June. What struck me as most poignant, out of that overload of information about one of the most heroic and horrific battles in history, was that so many of the young soldiers who landed on the beaches that became killing fields were seasick.

In this context, the old joke about the stages of motion sickness isn't very funny. You know, first you're afraid you're going to die, then you're afraid you're not. Some of the men who were tossed around by the English Channel in the steel boxes called landing craft surely died on Omaha and the other beaches because they were seasick.

The worst thing about this sailor's curse is not the nausea; it's the malaise that saps the will, turns arms and legs to rubber and overwhelms victims with the need to sleep. In this state, some people can't manage to wrap a line around a winch. Imagine wading into the gunfire on Normandy.

In sailing, motion sickness can be so debilitating that it evolves from a matter of discomfort to one of safety.

Afflicted sailors cope in various ways. The most successful manage it by having a good attitude. As in almost everything, a sense of humor goes a long way. Sailors who can visit the lee rail and return to their duties with a smile not only seem to get over it faster but are highly esteemed by their mates. I recall a crew-mate from a boisterous Atlantic passage. Even as the weather worsened, he munched cookies. After he made his inevitable trip to the lee rail, he announced with a laugh, "Just tossing my cookies," and took the helm.

Laughing at, rather than with, victims of *mal de mer* is another story. People who joke too strenuously about those who succumb to seasickness are not only insensitive but likely to fall into the trap of believing that what they are wont to call a "weak stomach" is the sign of a poor sailor. The truth is, great sailors, Admiral Nelson and Ted Turner among them, have been prone to suffer from the curse.

Those of the iron stomach set who fancy themselves immune should mind their hubris, for there is evidence that, when the motion gets crazy enough, everyone gets sick. Just ask the astronauts. None of them escaped seasickness when they were subjected to the torture of a fiendish motion machine in an attempt to prepare them for the sick-making environment of weightlessness in an orbiting space capsule.

But enough of this green-in-the-face stuff. It's not nearly as bad as it sounds. Most sailing is done in conditions where nobody gets sick. When sailors do get sick, especially on long offshore passages, the body, marvelous invention that it is, usually adjusts. The inner ear center of balance catches up, "sea legs" magically grow, and the motion is no longer agony but part of the joy of sailing.

For those who can't adjust, there are remedies. Ancient medicine provides acupuncture bands and ginger in various forms, both of which have adherents who swear to their effectiveness. Modern medicine provides strong drugs, whose sometimes annoying side effects are considered a small price to pay to kill the seasickness devil. Of the latter, the Transderm Scōp patch, the flesh-colored, dime-sized wafer of chemicals stuck to the skin behind the ear, has created a happy new class of born-again sailors.

Then there is this about seasickness: There is no greater indicator of the wonderfulness of sailing than the fact that people who have endured the misery of *mal de mer* slip on their boat shoes, zip up their foul weather gear and come back, again and again, to sail.

Sailing is Easy ...
No Kidding

JIM and Diana Jessie sailed for six years and tens of thousands of miles around the world on a big-rigged, 48-foot former racing yacht that does not have: an autopilot or self-steering gear; a roller furling headsail; a windlass; lazyjacks or other mainsail furling device.

"Look what it's done to me," graybearded, fiftysomething Jim says with a wink. "I'm really only 35 years old."

Jokes aside, these Californians who sailed away from busy, successful lives in Sausalito in 1985 don't look a bit the worse for having sailed so far and so long the old-fashioned way, which is to say the hard way. Call it hands-on sailing. Fact is, Jim and Diana's hands have been on the wheel of *Nalu IV* so much that they've worn through half a dozen elkhide wheel covers.

Even if she had the gadgets that most of today's cruising sailors would not leave the dock without, *Nalu* would be a handful for two. She was designed by Bill Lapworth and built by Bill Chapman 21 years ago of cold-molded plywood as a (by 1970 standards) light displacement ocean racing yacht that would sail with a crew of about 10.

Maybe the Jessies are just respecting *Nalu*'s racing heritage by keeping her free of cruising worksavers. Inveterate racers both, they have served as USYRU appeals judges and have sailed with some of the West Coast's best racing sailors. They've managed to keep their hands in competition by racing even while sailing around the world by taking part in races between such off-the-beaten-track ports of call as Darwin, Australia, and Ambon, Indonesia.

I thought of Jim and Diana, who are now bound for California via the Panama Canal, on a day when my mate and I would gladly have traded some of our boat's go-fast stuff for some good cruising gear. This was no Darwin to Ambon passage, mind you; just a 25-mile delivery after a weekend regatta. Jean and I left our crew on the dock and took off with a plan to cope with freshening head winds by leaving the sails down, the engine revved up and our spirits buoyed by the last of the beer, a leftover sandwich and some tunes from the cockpit speakers. Like a lot of my plans, this one went to hell in a hurry.

The breeze got stronger, the seas got bigger and our pretty red boat began to demonstrate why we sometimes call her *Red October*: Given a chance to go over a wave, she will invariably go through it. The cleaved wave then proceeds down the deck with a roar and assaults whomever is on deck or in the cockpit before exiting through the open transom. So much for the beer and sandwiches or the music, which was no longer audible.

We persevered. The engine didn't. The problem turned out to be water in the fuel. I sort of guessed that. There was water everywhere else—why not in the fuel tank? But this was no time to be fiddling with filters. It was time to—gulp!—raise the sails. That's what you do on sailboats, right?

You do—quite easily—if you have a mainsail handling system and a roller furling jib. We hard core racers, of course, have neither. That's because we think we go faster without them and because we have a gnarly image to maintain.

With the wind pushing 30 knots, the right combination for our boat would have been a reefed main and a number four jib. But I wouldn't have raised the main for all the Kevlar in captivity. Hoisting it wouldn't have been the problem. Reefing it might have been accomplished in less than an hour. Getting it down would have been easy. But controlling the beast (which in racing fashion is not attached to the mast) once it was on deck, to say nothing of flaking it on its 19-foot boom, would have challenged a dozen weight lifters.

So we would sail with just a headsail. With a furling headstay, we could have rolled out enough genoa to do the job in about 30 seconds. Instead, we spent 30 aerobically rewarding minutes setting a bulletproof heavy weather jib. The process started with dragging the sail forward and hooking up tack shackle, sheets and halyard and starting the head in the luff groove. No big deal, you say? Try it while sitting on the sail to keep it aboard *Red October* in full dive mode.

With the crew on board, the halyard would have been jumped at the mast and the sail would have been drawing in seconds. Without them, and with Jean having her hands full with the wheel, I sprinted back to grind away on the halyard winch. After three feet of sail were raised—not exactly in the wink of an eye; the self-tailer wasn't working, which is normal but hardly noticed when there are 11 people on board to pull strings—the luff fouled in the pre-feeder. This created a nice opportunity to go forward several times more to experience foredeck vertigo and straighten the board-like sail that the wind was folding as though it was part of an origami exercise.

The fore and aft commuting didn't stop when the sail reached full hoist. With the insane flapping the sheets had tied themselves into remarkably tight knots. I was able to sort out the problem in about the time it would take to read Dickens' **Bleak House**. But then, at last, we were sailing, rail down, full and by, drinking in the majesty of nature unleashed.

Actually, we would have preferred to have been drinking something else. After all the folderol, it was already cocktail hour and we were farther from home than when the engine fetched up.

That might have broken the spirits of less focused sailors, but our attitudes remained buoyant. Braced against the seas that invaded both the cockpit and our foul weather gear, we smiled gamely and shouted in one voice over the din of wave and wind, "God, isn't sailing great!"

Lest this account turn off anyone who may be considering sailing as a pleasant way to spend leisure time, I hasten to repeat that it doesn't have to be like this. People sail alone around the world without ever going forward to tend to headsails. In fact, gear to make sail handling easy has progressed so far that old racing sailors don't have to retire to powerboats anymore. When their passion for punishment cools, they can find a sturdy cruising sailboat with roll-up sails that is as easy to handle as any trawler.

Funny, the concept seems more intriguing than it used to be.

The Docking Nightmare

I USED to have this dream about docking.

In it, we sail the race of our lives. We finish just after some Maxi boats, whose owners are so in awe of our performance that they save us the place of honor at the dock in front of the yacht club. A grand crowd, decked out in blue blazers and white duck pants and bright dresses setting off golden tans and golden champagne in crystal that twinkles in the sun, is gathered on the clubhouse veranda for our arrival. As I swing the boat to back triumphantly into the stern-to mooring place between two elegant 80-footers, the crowd hushes and the Dixieland band stops playing midway through "The Saints Go Marching In." With a professional grace born of lifelong experience, I casually shift into reverse and gently rev the engine and … the damn boat goes sideways. The stern swings one way, the bow the other and the boats slams sideways into Maxi bows. Shards of exotic laminate fly like shrapnel, titanium pulpits bend like spaghetti. The crowd groans, crews lolling on the dock laugh derisively, the owners of the boats I've assaulted curse and I wake up.

I recalled the dream when a friend told me of his experiences docking a schooner in Bermuda, the prospect of which gave him stomach cramps and other symptoms of advanced anxiety.

Docking will do that to you. It may be the thing about sailing that people fear most. I've known sailors who could face the most unspeakably foul weather offshore without blinking an eye but got queasy at the thought of returning to shore and having to dock the boat.

It's not that handling a sailboat under power is all that hard. On a scale of difficulty it ranks just behind operating a Cuisinart. But it does involve some surprises—like what direction the boat will decide to go in reverse. I figure I stopped having the nightmare because I had experienced all the surprises, everything that can go wrong docking.

But I discovered a new one early this season in one of my first dockings of a new boat. The situation had the potential for a dicey landing—lots of wind, precious little turning space, a dock space between high-rise powerboats just long enough for the boat. The approach obviously needed a healthy jolt of speed. So I took aim and advanced the RPMs to something just shy of the vibration level that removes fillings. That was when the lever that controls both shift and throttle came off in my hand. If you've seen one of those old comedy movies, the ones where the steering wheel of the speeding car comes off and either Abbott or Costello is steering with a disconnected wheel, you have a rough idea of how I felt. Before my crew could jump overboard and the owner of the Hatteras that was about to be impaled by a very pointy sailboat could have a seizure, I managed to reinsert the handle in the tiny hole and put on the brakes with a shudder and a cloud of diesel smoke. Then I struck a cocky pose that said I always dock boats at hull speed.

That's the thing about docking—no matter how badly you screw up, you've got to look cool. Nonchalance can cover a multitude of docking disasters.

Docking can be as much a performance to impress an audience as a maneuver to bring a boat to land. Beemers (you know, BMWs, Boat Maintenance Workers, nee BNs), who have plenty of time to practice boat handling and a propensity for showing off, have it refined to an art. You can rate their work at regatta raft-ups. A typical nine-on-a-scale-of-ten performance would be backing an IOR Fifty at five knots through a swarm of boats, with the beemer having one hand on the 80-inch wheel and the other on the hip of a bikini-clad temporary crew person, into whose ear he is whispering as he brings the boat to a stop a fender's width from the dock.

Sometimes intimidation has a role in docking. I was a witness when an awfully big boat entered Chicago's Monroe Street harbor on a day when it was rolling with a nasty surge and was crisscrossed with lines holding boats, including mine, off the docks. When the visitor pointed at a favored dock space on the other side of the cat's cradle of lines, someone yelled, "You can't go there." The beemer helming the boat with studied nonchalance entoned in a loud, even voice: "Watch me!" Then he powered the Swan fiftysomething to his dock space just slowly enough for the onlookers to remove their lines.

One thing you can count on about docking is that there is usually plenty of help available, which is one of the main reasons people have trouble docking. Dockstanders love to take lines. Anyone who has ever docked a sailboat has met the helpful fellow who beckons for the bow line, catches it and instantly ties it down with a big granny knot as the boat coasts forward, inevitably bringing about an abrupt meeting of dock and hull. The only thing dockstanders like to do more than handling lines is giving docking advice. This should always be rejected, but often that's easier said than done.

I give my wife credit for the most creative and effective silencing of a dockside critic I've ever seen. She was on the foredeck to handle the bow line but was taking her time about it (because she wasn't quite sure which side we would tie on, because she had utter and complete faith in the highly competent person at the helm, and because we dock nonchalantly). The uptight dockmaster, probably irked because a cheapskate sailor was taking a place where a big-tipping powerboater might have docked, demanded that she "hurry up and throw me the line." Jean thought this was unreasonable and worse—it reeked of male superiority and sexist innuendo. So when he repeated it, she picked up a coil of unattached dock line and hurled it and a few words at him with impressive velocity. "There's your (expletive deleted) line," she said to the fellow with the coil of line on his chest. "Now what are you going to do with it?"

Well, that's all behind me now. I long ago unraveled the mysteries of sailboat docking and have more important things to worry about. As I write this I am preparing for the summer's biggest race, psyching myself to not only win a trophy but to finish early enough to get a slip, into which I will back with great style before an admiring audience.

Gulp.

Noisy Secrets of
the Owner's Stateroom

SOMEONE wrote that Dennis Conner spent three straight days below on *Winston* during the first leg of the Whitbread Race. I find it hard to believe. What could he have been doing? Certainly not sleeping. That's nigh onto impossible on a modern ocean racer for someone involved in the management of the boat. A business CEO can flee to his home or pied-a-terre, or lock the doors of a quiet office. A racing sailboat CEO can't hide from his problems. It's a matter of noise. Nothing conducts noise like a fiberglass hull.

On the old wooden sailing ships a captain's problem wasn't getting away from the action for a snooze but staying involved while ensconced in his well-insulated cabin. His solution was the telltale compass that hung over his berth to tell him if his ship was on course. Woe to the wheelsman who was caught by the captain's telltale compass steering west by southwest when the course was south by southwest.

The wooden ship helmsman, though, had a less stressful life than the sailors who steer and navigate a modern racing yacht while the skipper is in his bunk. The telltale compass has gone the way of manila rope; today's captains can take a handheld GPS to bed with them that will tell (in the dark) not only the course being steered but the boat's position and speed, where it should be going, how far away that is and how good a job the helmsman is doing getting there. With a gizmo like that telling tales, there are no secrets on a racing boat.

Not that there could be that many anyway on thin-hulled composite and fiberglass boats. Which is why I usually finish long distance races in need of a lengthy stay in a spa that specializes in restorative treatments for the sleep-deprived and chronically jetlagged. The problem is the noise.

The palatial owner's cabin on my boat is located under the cockpit; the berth is directly under a bank of winches. This arrangement, though less than ideal from a comfort standpoint, has the advantage of keeping the occupant of the cabin fully involved in the sail trimming process, which is a never ending process, a cleated sheet being anathema to a racing sailor. I've learned to recognize the various sail adjustments by their distinctive sounds. A squeak is a slight ease of the sheet. A groan accompanied by metallic clinking signals a sheet being trimmed in. High volume, long duration ratcheting sounds indicate a headsail being sheeted home after a tack. The anguished, piercing scream of rope being pulled off of a winch is the sound of a spinnaker trimmer letting the sheet go to prevent a broach. I know why they call the housing of a winch a drum—this machine has the ability to drive sound through fiberglass with the tympanic force of a kettle drum.

Winches are only one part of this orchestra. A dropped winch handle detonates an explosive report in any ears that happen to be under the cockpit sole. The movement of numerous crew feet, as in, say, the cockpit ballet required by a spinnaker jibe, generates a cacophony that is probably not unlike the last sounds heard by someone trampled by a herd of wildebeests.

Kept awake by the infernal noise, the reclining skipper has ample opportunity to worry himself into a frazzle about the progress of the race, while listening in on the conversation of the on-watch that filters through the fiberglass with the clarity of a CIA telephone tap. This dialogue further staves off any threat of sleep by its potential to unravel the skipper's brilliant strategic plan to win the race—as when the watch captain announces to his mates, "Good, he's finally outta here, let's get over on port tack where we belong."

Incipient mutiny like that should get the captain out of his cabin in a hurry, but there's one noise down there that is sometimes worth staying for. This sound comes not from sources on the boat but from outside of it, through the plastic hull as though by some magic resonance. It is the timeless noise of sailing, the melody made by the duet of hull and water, a pure sound of nature, replete with primal power, untainted by engine drone or propeller vibration or other human racket.

The symphony of water playing on a moving hull can be such a reliable speedometer that a skipper in his berth doesn't need to check his telltale GPS. The sound-speed scale starts with the dreaded no-sound-at-all level—becalmed, dead in the water— and progresses to the two-knot whisper of bubbles, the busy gurgling of the four-knot level, the aggressive rushing water sound of six knots, followed by an acceleration of liquidy decibels through the roar of hull speed to the overwhelming din of a hull being pushed through the water beyond its theoretical speed limit.

To a sailor bent on sailing fast, these are sweet sounds. Sometimes they put me to sleep.

The Language of Docking

TO me it's Greek. The best language, that is, to use while docking a sailboat in adverse conditions.

Greek is a complex and powerful tool of expression, with its rich Mediterranean vowel sounds and rolling diphthongs interspersed with hard-hitting consonants. By adroitly changing inflection and speed a Greek speaker can deliver a withering oral assault, which is an important part of docking, especially in Greece.

Greek, of course, is an ancient language, but I have a theory that its spoken power evolved in recent times, just since boats started mooring stern-to in the Greek islands.

I propounded this theory after studying docking practices in some of the harbors of the Aegean islands while cruising with friends and Markos Voutsinos, a native son of the island of Siros. I concluded that such docking would be impossible without fluency in Greek.

There's more to it than the language of stern-to mooring, of course. Proper equipment, for example. Markos has all the right stuff on the custom Jeanneau 56-footer he skippers for GPSC Charters, including a 90 horsepower engine and a substantial three-bladed propeller (for assertive backing), 10 heavy-duty fenders (for self-defense) and a 75-pound CQR anchor at the end of many fathoms of three-eighths inch chain (for security and intimidation).

The ground tackle may sound like something you would use to anchor for an evening at Cape Horn, but as a wily survivor of the docking wars Markos knows it's right at home in the sunny harbors of Greece. For one thing, the winds are weird there—they can go from zero to 60 faster than a Corvette. And for another, this oversize gear is needed to daunt would-be trespassers.

Markos' modus operandi is to drop the hook as far from the dock as possible for maximum scope, then back the boat, bristling with fenders on both sides, vigorously amid the cacophony of clattering chain and revving engine, putting on the brakes and tying up exactly the length of the gangplank away from the dock. Then comes the hard part: Markos stands guard, ready to defend his space against interlopers who would barge in where there isn't room.

The most easily rebuffed intrusions are from bareboat charterers, like the naive Frenchman who drops a lightweight anchor on a rubberbandy nylon rode close to the dock. Without heavy chain to hold his bow in the cross breeze, he backs sideways on course to fetch up on the forest green topsides of the boat Markos is sworn to protect.

A short, loud burst of Greek does the trick. The Frenchman can't understand a word of what Markos is saying, but communication is perfect—he instantly gets the idea he's not being welcomed to a rafting party. Chastened, he lifts his puny anchor and moves on. Markos sends him on his way with some good natured advice in French.

The arrival of a charter boat in the charge of a Greek captain with designs on the sliver of space between our hull and our starboard neighbor presents a more formidable challenge. This guy is armed—he talks Greek.

The antagonists are both Greek professional skippers, but there the similarity ends. Markos has sailed the equivalent of five or six times around the world, but he's still very much the island boy, barefoot, dressed in jeans and *SAILING* Magazine T-shirt, tan face wreathed in wild, ink-colored hair. His middle-aged adversary is dressed like a yachtsman and actually wears a Greek fisherman's hat like they sell in the tourist shops in Athens.

Markos issues the challenge with a barked fusillade of Greek words. The other captain answers in kind. So far, it's a draw.

The intruder backs on, intent on squeezing into this prime but too-small spot on the quay at Hydra. Markos peppers him with more Greek. He comes back with louder Greek, emphasized with gestures, but while he's distracted the boat stops. The rudder is fouled in an anchor rode. Markos smiles.

While the intruder climbs down the stepped transom and pokes at the offending rode with a boat hook, Markos keeps up an unrelenting patter of (no doubt insulting) Greek. He gesticulates toward the unfolding fiasco, rolls out a chain of Greek words with an inflection that now suggests ridicule. He involves some Greek speaking bystanders, including the hirsute, tattooed harbormaster who wears a greasy Cincinnati Reds hat, as bit players in what now has the makings of a theatrical production. Soon the air is so full of Greek words you can almost see the Greek letters, the sharp deltas and sigmas, the rounded omegas and all the rest, falling down on the frustrated captain.

It is splendid chaos. Some of us hold off the intruding boat. Markos and his kibitzers chatter on. The charterers seem to be edging toward the bow of their boat to get away from the source of the conflict. A small crowd gathers in front of the nearest waterfront taverna to follow the drama. Suddenly the captain fixes Markos with a murderous look, points the boat hook at him and shouts ...

Incredibly, what he shouts isn't Greek. He shouts an American expletive, the ever popular "F" word, three times, followed by the word "off." I know instantly the battle is over. That four-letter classic may be the most powerful obscenity in the English language, but it's a wimpy rejoinder to Greek.

His cool blown, the would-be intruder has nothing left to do but clear his rudder and slink off to a far corner of the harbor to tie up behind a rust-stained caique freighter.

It's a good thing we don't do stern-to mooring in the U.S. Our language isn't up to it.

Fly the Flag Properly
and Watch the Salsa

NO one stepped in the salsa, but it was a close thing. The salsa was in a bowl in the middle of the cockpit, resting, in the embrace of haystacks of tortilla chips, on a cooler filled with various libations, surrounded by men and women happily engaged in one of the hallowed rituals of sailing. The sun had dipped below the yardarm, or was at least in the region of the top spreader, glasses were filled and the main brace was about to be properly spliced. It was cocktail hour.

Then they came, like a flying wedge on a kickoff return team, three bulky guys carrying bulky duffel bags, careening through the cockpit, the party and very nearly the salsa. "Sorry, gotta get to the boat next door," the lead blocker explained helpfully.

First rule of rafting etiquette: When crossing over boats in a raft, always pass in front of the main mast.

I hesitate to use the E-word, for fear it will revive goofy perceptions of sailing as a rich person's recreation practiced in blue blazers and white hats or some such mufti. Still, sailors over the years have figured out the right way to do things and, though the term may sound stuffy, these are yachting traditions worth following.

Most of them must be learned by experience and common sense, because they are not written. An exception is nautical flag etiquette, which has been prescribed in text for ages. It may seem like dry stuff, but the American flag can be an incendiary subject, even when the issue is not flag-burning.

When the small town that is my home port opened a new marina, the harbormaster ran up a grand display of flags on a proper nautical pole. A burgee went to the top; the 50-star national flag flew proudly from the peak of the gaff. All hell broke loose.

Flag-wavers packed the city council chamber and demanded that Old Glory be flown from the top of the pole, nautical flag etiquette be damned. Among a flurry of letters to the editor of the local newspaper on the subject was one suggesting that yacht owners were too consumed by their expensive toys to appreciate patriotism.

Today, the American flag flies from the top of the marina pole—where, by the time-honored rules of flag etiquette, it definitely does not belong.

The author of the letter to the editor had it wrong, of course. Boat owners wave the flag with the best of them. Problem is, though, that, unlike the harbormaster who knew his flag etiquette, many of them don't seem to have a clue about how to do it.

In the past sailing season, I have seen American flags flying from: backstays, mastheads, headstays and spreaders. The latter would be appropriate on a sailboat visiting from, say, Rovinj, Croatia, but not an American registered boat, for that is the place for courtesy flags on visiting foreign yachts. The other flag flying locations mentioned are not acceptable under any circumstances.

The most remarkable flag faux pas I observed was a display hoisted on a jib halyard tacked at the stem featuring the American flag as the top flag in a string that included a Mount Gay rum banner, a yacht club burgee and numerous racing brag flags. As if to magnify the breach of etiquette, the American flag was the size of a tarp adequate to cover a good-sized boat, perhaps indicating that the owner thought that patriotism is measured by the square foot. Nothing short of a gale could stir the outsized flag, and it drooped like a tired tent over the motley assortment of flags beneath it.

There is a rule covering flag size on boats. Ironically, it is usually cited to discourage flying a flag that is too small, but it works both ways. It says the width of a flag should be one inch for every foot of boat length. I reckoned that the version of the Stars and Stripes I saw flying with the brag flags on a 40-foot racer-cruiser was the right size for a 160-foot boat.

Where, when and how should the flag be flown on a sailboat? A good guide is John Rousmaniere, who in his **The Annapolis Book of Seamanship** interprets the traditional etiquette in a way that takes into account the requirements of contemporary boats: The ensign (the 50-star national flag) or the yacht ensign (the nautical version with 13 stars and a fouled anchor) may be flown from the traditional position stitched to the leech of the aftermost sail or from a staff at the stern. It should be flown from 8 a.m. to sunset when under way or when anchored or moored, but not when racing. The club burgee should be flown at the masthead on a pigstick or, if that's not practical because of the clutter common on modern mastheads, at the starboard, lowermost spreader.

Deviations from these rules are hardly cause to alert the American Legion; let's not add the offense of making the American flag share a halyard with brag flags to the desecrations covered by the proposed Flag Protection Amendment. But ignorance of flag etiquette on sailboats is a shame because pleasure boats have been given a special role in the display of the American flag acknowledged by tradition and recognized by law.

And it is a shame because there are few more glorious ways to show America's beautiful national symbol than on a sailboat—standing proudly out from a staff or, in a sight to take your breath away, on a gaff-rigged yacht, rail down in a fresh breeze, with that brilliant patch of red, white and blue waving exuberantly from the leech of the mainsail.

If I may return briefly to a more mundane issue of sailing etiquette, I would like to make it clear that we do welcome rafters, rafting being one of the appealing social aspects of sailing. In fact, rafters, join our party and have some salsa and chips. Just come by way of the front of the mast.

A Fair Wind?
Don't Count on It

CONTROL freaks need not apply. Sailing is not for people who have to be in control—because the essential ingredient of sailing is uncontrollable, not to mention maddening and unreliable. I'm talking about wind.

Wind has driven sailors nuts forever. We love it, we have to have it, but we can't get enough of it. Or we get too much of it. Or we get the right amount of it from the wrong direction.

Sailors have no monopoly on this. Wind has been driving people in general nuts forever. Literally. They say people start acting crazy if the Santa Ana, the hot northeast wind that sears California, blows too long. A number of cultures call their indigenous versions of the Santa Ana "poison winds" because of their toxic effect on mind and body.

Like mythical gods, important winds have names: mistral, williwaw, melteme, simoom, sirocco, chinook and many more less well known.

If some winds can make you sick, others can bring a cure. For example, the Fremantle doctor. The Indian Ocean seabreeze made famous by the 1987 America's Cup series is well named. At midday, just as the heat of the Western Australian coast rises from miserable to intolerable, the doctor makes its house call, and everyone is refreshed, especially sailors, who can play in the doctor-induced seas and 20-plus knot breeze.

As in most temperate zone coastal areas, the place where I do most of my summer sailing has a version of the doctor. It's considerably less aggressive—maybe it's a nurse or a paramedic. But it does the job, bringing relief for the sweltering on shore and for wind-starved sailors at sea.

The seabreeze is a likable wind because it's more or less predictable. On sunny summer days, the land heats up, warm air rises, and cool air from the adjacent sea fills the vacuum, at about the same time every day and from the same direction.

Weather systems are sluggish in summer, so for days on end the only wind might be that afternoon thermal breeze. This is part of the contrariness of wind—when we need it most, during the sailing season, it's scarce. I ruminate about this fairly often in the off-season as I pound the pavement on the old familiar route of my daily run, first cruising downwind along Lake Shore Road and then beating back into the teeth of a biting north wind that is usually strong enough to require a good bit of body lean. As frozen breath turns my mustache into what probably looks to passing motorists like a miniature snowdrift under my nose, I conclude that it isn't fair that all of this wind is wasted on winter.

Sailors like to talk about fair winds, but wind isn't fair. Everyone who has raced a sailboat knows that. If wind were fair no one would ever experience the nightmare of sailing the good race, leaving the competition behind, and then, in sight of the finish, falling into a windless hole from which, with stomach-churning dread, you watch the sails of the boats you had beaten climb over the horizon and inevitably, in their own private and totally undeserved breeze, sail by. This is one of the most excruciating forms of psychic hell and is why you should not carry firearms on board.

Memories of visiting this hell lead me to suggest that having too little wind is worse than having too much, but then I've never sailed in a hurricane. From that vantage point, a windless hole would probably have a certain appeal. I have sailed in squalls, of course, and I suppose some of them have had a few minutes of hurricane force wind. Of all the manifestations of wind, squalls may be the most magnificent.

In daylight (squalls shouldn't be allowed at night, but then wind isn't fair) squalls telegraph their approach with one of nature's most thrilling and menacing displays: that white wall of a cloud that seems to boil the water, rolling out of a tar black sky fractured by golden bolts of lightning. It's the sort of thing that can transfix a sailor, in the manner of a deer frozen in headlights. Even those who are able to move swiftly to prepare can be surprised. No matter how often I've experienced it, the fury of the instant maelstrom is shocking. Still, squalls are sometimes welcome because, after all, they are wind.

I have a friend who, peering at his fancy new radar screen during a long distance race, spotted what he identified as a squall. He sailed quite far out of his way to take advantage of this rich source of strong wind and finally reached the radar image—where he sat becalmed for an hour in an utterly windless deluge.

Chalk it up as yet another of the frustrations of wind. They are so numerous that is best not to dwell on them. The happy sailor is one who comes to terms with the vagaries of the wind and understands the folly of thinking the wind should blow from the southwest because he is sailing north. The happiest sailor is the one who just goes where the wind blows him.

The Immersion Test

REMEMBER when the British Virgin Islands were exotic?

That was when bareboat chartering was new and sailors discovered that the paradise they had read about and the Cane Garden Bay they had heard Jimmy Buffett sing about were suddenly accessible to those without the means or the inclination to rent a luxury yacht and liveried crew.

The BVI haven't changed much since the time they were exotic. They still rank among the best places on earth to sail. But the growth of bareboat chartering, one of the signal developments in the progress of sailing, has raised the standard for the exotic designation. Exotic now is Fiji, Tahiti, the islands of Australia and beyond. This faraway exotica, once mainly the stuff of sailors' dreams, is now an easily grasped reality.

I suppose there are some exotic sailing destinations where the water is cloudy and cold, but I'll put those at the bottom of my list of places to sail. In ranking the appeal of a sailing place, wind, sun, warmth, the people, the land, flora and fauna count, but the character of the water is what makes the difference. You know you are in cruising nirvana when you can see your anchor 50 feet down.

For my part, I rate the success of a cruise by the amount of time spent in, rather than on, the water. I know I'm sailing in the right part of the world if I can start and end each day with a swim and spend plenty of time in between in an immersed state.

I've been told by a dear cruising companion that I am border-line obsessive about the swimming thing. Maybe so, but I've been doing it since well before I started reading the Patrick O'Brian series, so it's not a matter of aping the books' hero, the redoubtable Capt. Jack Aubrey, who is wont to dive off his war-ship for a salutary dip whenever the urge strikes him, even, to the astonishment of his crew, when the vessel is under sail.

At any rate, the exotic cruising grounds mentioned above meet the immersion standard admirably and so, of course, does most of the Caribbean.

I say most because of the still fresh memory of the time we sailed into the bay of Fort de France, Martinique, and dropped the anchor rather close to shore. Without looking around, I took my plunge, trying to make sort of a showy dive. When I surfaced, it was not to the applause of my crewmates but to looks that ranged from disgusted to horrified. I had performed by ablution within a hundred yards of the gaping mouth of the island's vast sewage canal.

On closer inspection, I couldn't see my big toe in the water off Fort de France, much less the anchor. Not that clarity is a fool-proof test of swimability. On a spring boat delivery on Lake Superior, I became mesmerized by water so perfectly limpid that it magnified individual grains of sand on the distant bottom. My dive snapped me back to the reality that the human body was not made to be immersed in 42-degree Fahrenheit liquid.

All of this swimming tends to dilute the importance of that American ritual, the daily shower. Boat people seem to have a particular affinity for this exercise. I make that statement based on a phenomenon I've observed during nonexotic, coastwise, mainland cruising. People park their boats, often magnificent craft worth far more than the owners' homes and surely equipped with all amenities, including showers, jump off with dopp kit and hair dryer in hand and rush to the marina head to queue up for a shower. It doesn't seem to matter that at busy marinas these facilities soon achieve a level of squalor that would be unacceptable in a military barrack or high school locker room. I guess one of the appeals of this kind of cruising is its nostalgic resemblance to summer camp.

Many sailors consider the first shower ashore after a long showerless passage to be one of life's great pleasures. I remember my longest time at sea without a shower. The shore shower that followed it was indeed a wonderful thing, but it wasn't something I yearned for during the boisterous winter passage. Getting wetter, what with the ocean coming aboard regularly and the skies opening frequently, didn't seem all that appealing at the time. Offending others with deteriorating personal hygiene wasn't an issue—we were never out of foul-weather gear. When I think back, what I dreamed of on those long cold watches was not a shower—it was a martini.

On many of today's cruising boats, the showers are so good that they rival shore facilities. I sailed on a 47-foot charter boat recently that had no less than four roomy, stand-up shower stalls and enough freshwater capacity to keep them going the duration of the cruise.

Still, my idea of a great cruise is the one on which you don't need a shower. Just call me Capt. Jack.

When Sailors Fall for
the Siren Song of Twin V-8s

IT'S not quite like a death in the family. More like the sudden conversion of a lifelong Green Bay Packer backer into a Chicago Bears fan. Or the overnight switch by a dyed-in-the-wool Republican to the Democratic party. Or Mother Teresa announcing she has been named CEO of General Motors. In other words, not tragic, but shocking. I am referring to the decision by friends of mine—two couples—to sell their sailboats and buy power-boats.

This is momentous, for these folks have been sailors for as long as I have known them. They are members in good standing of a group of kindred spirits whose summer lives are focused on their sailboats, who have stacked up the memories of happy times sailing together.

Other members of the group have been good-natured about the sea change in their friends' lives. There have been only a few jokes about exchanging sturdy sailors' foul weather gear for such glitzy powerboating garb as yachtsman's hats encrusted with faux gold braid and coils of gold neck chains. For my part, I have restrained myself from disparaging comments about such motor-boat essentials as stereophonic loud hailers and chrome fender racks, and haven't said a word about powerboats polluting the water and air and hurting lovable manatees.

We're being kind because, while we might not agree with their decision, we respect it. There are things, after all, to be said for powerboats. For one, they go faster than sailboats, not an insignificant advantage in times when it is verging on the socially unacceptable to take the time to enjoy leisure at a leisurely pace. They also can be parallel parked with comparative ease and can be operated from dry, protected, heated and air conditioned spaces while watching television and eating quiche. What's more, they can actually make progress directly into the wind; they do this without heeling.

Still, when good sailors with a long commitment to the sailing ethic fall for the siren song of speed, comfort, convenience and freedom from tacking, it can shake the confidence of the saltiest sailor. It prompted me to examine my conscience to see if I am still a true believer. It turns out I am. (I guess I can keep my job.) If you believe in the following credo, you are too.

Sailing is beautiful. It is true that beauty is in the eye of the beholder, and that people who have beheld trucks, house trailers, manure spreaders and powerboats have pronounced them beautiful. But the beauty of a sailboat transcends an enthusiast's bias. There is a reason sailboats, even dry-docked or anchored, but especially under sail when they combine fluid curves and bold angles with grace in motion, so inspire photographers, artists and writers: They are among the most beautiful manmade objects extant. It is a privilege to be near such beauty.

Sailing is benign. It takes nothing from nature and gives nothing back. A sailboat can enter and leave a perfect marine wilderness without leaving behind so much as a faint footprint to record its passing. There is a balance here. Sailing depends on nature, and it is kind to it in turn.

Sailing challenges us. Sailing is more than a beautiful, benign form of recreation; it is also art, craft and science. It is easily learned by beginners, but good sailors never stop learning. Each outing, each passage is an opportunity, should we choose to use it, to polish our sailing skills, whether they be in the timeless arts of seamanship or the newest wrinkles of sail trimming. These opportunities add to the plain joys of sailing, of moving over the sea with only the sounds of the waves and the wind. To sail is a higher order of achievement than to drive a car—or a powerboat.

Sailing lets us dream. Sailing is a romance created out of the heroic deeds and brave explorations, the discoveries and circumnavigations, the glorious adventures of sailors through the ages. We are sailors like them. We may sail in their wakes. Or we may never leave our watery backyards, for lack of time or money or even nerve, but we can dream.

It's a pity my newly empowered friends are going to miss all of that, but the speed and comfort will compensate somewhat, and I'm sure they'll enjoy this summer's group cruise. I might sail along—I'm starting to see the advantages of cruising in company with powerboaters. They can scope out anchorages or reserve slips, and have the grills fired up by time the sailors arrive. And since my boat carries a fairly small supply of water, I'll be looking forward to a hot shower in a spacious powerboat bathroom. Or do they have Jacuzzis?

GPS is Nearly Perfect,
but It's Not Fair

I am trying to resist curmudgeonly temptations. But I want in the worst way to demand that someone pass a draconian law requiring boat operators to learn dead reckoning and celestial navigation before they are allowed to use a pocket-size gizmo that can tell any dummy exactly where in the world he is. I want this not because it's likely anyone will ever need these skills again. I want it because we ancient mariners of the pre-GPS era endured the frustration of never really knowing where we were and, dammit, new sailors should know what it feels like.

I realize I am exhibiting the unseemly instinct that has kept rites of initiation popular through the ages, but I can't help it. Allowing a neophyte to use GPS without serving time navigating the old way is like letting a recruit wear a spiffy military uniform without suffering through basic training, or letting a fraternity pledge use the secret handshake without going through hell week.

It's just the unfairness of it all. GPS navigating is so easy, so cheap, so good, so very nearly perfect that new "navigators" (draw your own conclusions as to why the quotation marks are there) are better on their first day at sea than we veterans of the dark age before the sky was full of man-made stars were after years of practice. Worst of all, they might never know about the hardships we endured.

So I say let them experience a landfall without knowing what land they're falling on. Let them emerge from the fog to see an unfamiliar shore and have to flip a coin to decide whether to turn right or left to find their destination. Let them resort to a quaint publication called a Light List in a desperate attempt to identify lights winking on the horizon to provide a clue to where they might be. Let them listen for a fog horn to find a harbor entrance. Let them turn into their bunks unsecure in the knowledge that their sextant fix is not an exact position but a hopeful indication that their boat is in a general area of the ocean the size of a large city. Let them, for a final exam, try to find their position on a rough, wet night by listening to the coded beeps of a radio direction finder.

I know, the last one is unfair. I'm not sure if radio beacons even exist any more. Not that it matters. As far as I know, no one has ever successfully triangulated a usable position by RDF anyway. Still, it would be a character-building exercise.

Those of us who are initiated members of the Order of Dead Reckoners can at least take comfort in the knowledge that we can help ourselves to the rich rewards of GPS without guilt. Those rewards became even richer at 12:04 a.m. EDT May 2, 2000, when the government turned off selective availability—the small error applied to GPS fixes for military security purposes. GPS positions are now accurate to something like 50 feet.

If everything worked as well as the Global Positioning System, there would be few problems left to solve in this world. Which is all the more amazing when you consider that the federal government created it. Our tax dollars at work—splendidly for a change. The U.S. Defense Department spent $12 billion to put 24 satellites and a network of ground stations in place. Anyone with a receiver can access the satellites' information for free.

Thanks to the American free enterprise system, the story gets better. The first GPS receiver I owned had a retail price of $9,995. I have one now that you can buy for $100 and change. It is about the size of a candy bar and does more than the 10 grand unit, which was the size of a microwave oven.

The leap from exotic hardware to ubiquitous gadget has gone so far that GPS receivers are now sometimes given away as premiums. That's how I got my handheld model. All I had to do was test drive a Cadillac. My friend the dealer knew I wasn't Cadillac material—I'm at least 10 years and 30 pounds away from needing a land yacht—but he cheerfully gave me the keys to a Seville. I drove it around the block, and in a few weeks General Motors sent me a nice GPS unit.

The theory, if not the hardware, of GPS is elegantly simple. The receiver catches signals beamed at the speed of light from satellites 11,000 miles away. The position of the satellites is known. The time it takes a signal to reach a receiver is measured. With signals from three satellites and fourth to correct mistakes in time measurement a position can be triangulated, almost instantly, nearly perfectly.

It isn't foolproof. I know of a man who started a cruise on his new 30-foot sailboat by setting his autopilot to steer to the GPS waypoint of his first destination, thinking in his blissful ignorance that his GPS was smart enough to set a course around an intervening point. It wasn't.

The Global Positioning system has never failed, but I suppose it could. It is conceivable that it could be turned off. Instead of degrading accuracy to discourage an enemy from using the system against U.S. forces, the military is working on what it calls "regional denial capabilities." If you happen to be sailing in a region where the system is denied, it's back to dead reckoning.

Well, I'm ready. I have my Light List, my plastic sextant and a dim memory of recording speed and distance and set and drift. I even have a RDF. I saved it as a talisman against navigator's hubris. Just looking at the silly thing reminds me that we once actually went sailing without knowing where we were.

Following the School Bus
to a meeting with the Mexican

THE rewards of sailboat racing transcend the fun of competition. Consider the aesthetics, for example. There are beautiful things to see and experience on the race course. One is the most elegant maneuver in sailing, the spinnaker jibe.

The sail, a voluptuous cloth sculpture, stands full against the sky as the boat turns. With balletic nimbleness, the bowperson swings the pole through the foretriangle and attaches a new guy as it passes by. Choreographed trimmers adjust the foreguy, afterguy and sheet. Smoothly turning beneath the taut spinnaker, always moving at speed, the boat effortlessly assumes a new course with the wind on a different side. In all, a seamless exercise in graceful motion.

Even taking down the flamboyant sail we nickname chute or kite can be a thing of beauty, though when I began racing the spinnaker drop was not such a pretty sight. The practice in those days was to release the tack, let the sail stream aft, inch the halyard down and laboriously gather the sail into the cockpit. You knew the maneuver was not successful when you saw a boat proceeding up the windward leg with a large, oddly shaped flag streaming from the masthead.

Once sailors learned that spinnakers do not have to obey the law of gravity, things changed. Now spinnakers are dropped by simply letting the halyard go. The sail hovers magically on a cushion of air over the water as the gently undulating mass of gaudy cloth waits patiently to be pulled under the headsail and onto the foredeck.

The perfect jibe and float takedown are particularly satisfying to view from the helm. Alas, the view for me has changed, for we sail now with asymmetric spinnakers. These sails, flown from a retractable, bowspritlike pole, are superior to conventional spinnakers in a number of ways—yes, after only a few weeks of sailing with them, I am a true believer—but elegance in handling maneuvers is not one of them.

Take the jibe. This is somewhat like politics or sausage in that you really don't want to know what goes into it. The one ingredient I have identified is a tremendous amount of pulling—mighty tugging on the leech, furious winch grinding. While a symmetric spinnaker with the standard two clews and a head rides through the jibe majestically above it all, the asymmetric is dragged kicking and screaming around the headstay, its gorgeous form momentarily destroyed as it is literally turned inside out. It doesn't take much longer than a conventional spinnaker jibe, but when observed from the back of the boat the process seems endless. When the sail finally fills on the new jibe with a satisfying snap, the sense of relief is akin to that of leaving the dentist's chair after a root canal.

Because of their geometry and the fact that they are flown from deck level, asymmetrics are bigger than comparable conventional spinnakers. On our boat, the biggest spinnaker resides in a rectangular bag that could sleep half the crew if it were a tent. The stuffed container is too big to pass through any hatch or companionway. It is also bright yellow with black lettering. Hence, the crew has named it and the sail it contains the "School Bus."

Crews handling a spinnaker like the School Bus should not be tempted by the beauty of the float takedown. Using this method is a good way to take a break from sailboat racing to go fishing by trawling a large, colorful net. The better alternative is to take the spinnaker down on the windward side of the genoa.

Except for a free rum party, nothing attracts sailors as quickly as a fellow sailor clawing his way up a learning curve. So I've received plenty of free advice on the handling of asymmetric spinnakers. One acquaintance recommended that we coat every inch of every spinnaker with a spray lubricant to cut friction during the sticky voyage around the headstay. This makes a lot of sense. The only reason we haven't done it yet is that it's a somewhat daunting project. An analogy of spray-painting a football field comes to mind.

The best tip on takedowns came from Buddy Melges, which stands to reason since he is not only the oracle on all matters of yacht racing but knows asymmetrics inside and out from his experience on the eponymous Melges 24 and 30 rockets. When Buddy confided, "Bill, you've got to use the Mexican," I said "gracias" and took the advice.

It turned out that this was not a plug for ethnic diversity in yacht racing crews. Rather, Buddy was recommending a takedown method in which the boat approaches a port-rounded mark on starboard tack, jibes near the mark and drops the spinnaker on the windward side of the headsail.

All right, it isn't quite that easy. Foredeck people (as many as you can find) have to encourage the spinnaker to fall into the jib but keep it from blowing into the mast. At some point, the sheet is eased, but not the tack. The halyard has to be released gradually in concert with the jibing genoa.

What's more, the helmsman has to turn the boat at just the right speed to keep the spinnaker on the windward side. If you ask me, this is a lot of pressure to put on someone who is used to blaming the people on the bow for botched takedowns. If the helmsman messes up, or anything else goes wrong, the likelihood of which rises in direct proportion to the wind velocity, the sail falls not on the foredeck but on the water, where it can endanger the coho salmon population.

During a Mexican takedown, the boat has to point straight downwind for a bit. The name was coined at the 1992 America's Cup at San Diego, where because of the prevailing wind, the boats were always pointed at Mexico during the takedown.

In the regatta in which we first tried the Mexican takedown, we were always pointed at a city on the other side of Lake Michigan, so we renamed it the Muskegon.

Whatever you call it, the windward takedown and other spinnaker-handling challenges are a small price to pay for the scintillating performance of asymmetrics. It's intoxicating stuff when the School Bus is filling the sky and the boat is following it to the leeward mark at double-digit speeds. Of course, this is balanced by the sobering thought that at these speeds the mark comes up in a hurry, which hastens the arrival of another risky rendezvous with the Mexican.

Polemics of Sail

It's Getting Harder
to Sail Away from
our Nanny

WE like to blame Big Brother, but the real source of the regulations that are creeping ever farther out on the water these days is little cousins, ordinary folks, citizens who just can't abide too much freedom. These well-intentioned people get together in what are known as grass-roots organizations and work to make the world safer for all of us.

Currently a grass-roots organization is campaigning for legislation to require guards on boat engine propellers, even on small outboards such as those used as auxiliary power on many sailboats.

The idea is to protect people from propeller injuries. How serious is this threat to the safety of boaters? Serious enough that a Texas law firm specializing in personal injury lawsuits has devoted a Web page to it. I don't know if this constitutes trolling for business, but I did read that, in the opinion of a company that provides expert court testimony, trolling motor props are among the worst offenders.

I don't mean to make light of propeller injuries, which like many things that can happen to us can be terrible. But do they warrant yet another boating regulation?

The Coast Guard tried to answer that question. The trade

magazine *Boating Industry International* reported that SPIN, a grass-roots organization whose perfect acronym stands for Stop Propeller Injuries Now, pressed the Coast Guard to do something about propellers. The agency responded by creating a Propeller Strike Prevention Regulation Project and appointing a civilian manager, who searched boating accident statistics for evidence of a need for regulation. He concluded there is no such need after finding, according to the magazine, that the "annual number of fatalities caused by prop strikes was two, five and one in 1995, 1996 and 1997."

Fatalities of any number should be taken seriously, of course, but these numbers seem to put prop strikes in the realm of lightning strikes, in which the result can be awful but the odds aren't that bad.

Speaking of lightning, do you think a grass-roots organization advocating a regulation requiring a lightning dissipating device on every masthead is next?

Forgive me if this is coming across as flippant—believe me, I'm a big supporter of safety, at sea, on highways, in bathrooms, everywhere—but the assaults on the liberty that has always been associated with sailing are getting to the point where one either laughs or cries. In a matter of months we've seen efforts to require everyone who operates a boat to be licensed and to make the wearing of PFDs mandatory. On top of that, there is now talk of trying to make it illegal for anyone operating a boat to drink alcohol.

A grass-roots organization called BADD (an appropriate acronym, in my opinion, and not because it stands for Boaters Against Drunk Driving) is proselytizing on behalf of the notion that skippers should not drink alcohol, not a single beer, not a single drop.

BADD means to do good, of course. Drunken boat operators cause accidents that hurt and kill people. Prohibition, it says, is the remedy.

Here we go again: Take away the freedom of everyone because a few can't handle it.

Here's a better way: Punish only those who are causing the problem. Existing laws (.08 or .10 percent blood alcohol level in most states and .10 percent in federal waters) already prohibit drunken boating. Better enforcement by local authorities in state waters where most accidents occur, and not prohibition, is what is needed.

I don't think we'll be seeing any zero-tolerance drinking laws soon. Even BADD says it's merely trying to make skippers voluntarily take the pledge. But as part of the trend of escalating regulation of our lives on the water, talk of bluenose drinking laws is creepy.

What you'll notice about this trend is that its genesis is in powerboats. Sailors aren't the problem, but we certainly are affected by it and its attempted solutions. The incompetent boat handling that inspires the licensing campaign, the accident statistics that power the mandatory PFD drive, the ghastly collisions with other boats or breakwaters that fuel the anti-drinking push all rise in direct proportion to horsepower.

Sailboats, under wind or propeller power, are so slow they're the butt of jokes (you know, watching grass grow or paint dry). Yet they demand no small amount of skill and effort to operate, and thus sailors tend to be serious students of seamanship and boat handling. The rewards of sailing are the satisfaction of mastering its disciplines and savoring its glorious aesthetics, not the imagined testosterone boost of neck-snapping acceleration or thunderous exhaust roar. All reasons why the cloak of overweening rules of behavior doesn't fit sailors.

Most of all, it doesn't fit sailors because what draws many to sailing is the ability to sail away for a time from a society that increasingly acts like an intrusive nanny who knows what's best for us to a world where self-reliance rules.

That world still exists, but we have to sail ever farther off-shore to find it.

In the world closer to shore, sailors may need a grass-roots self-defense organization.

Pay-Per-Rescue an Affront to Sailors

OUT of the corner of an eye, the rest of which was reading a newspaper, I caught an image of a sailboat moving across the television screen on the nightly news. I looked up to see that it was a 35 or 40-footer carrying storm canvas in big seas. When an orange helicopter moved into the picture, I assumed I was watching a breaking news report of a rescue at sea. It turned out it was file footage promoting an upcoming feature. The voice-over by Tom Brokaw said the report would expose how taxpayers were being ripped off paying for the rescue of yachtsmen by the United States Coast Guard.

The ensuing piece contained sound bites from people who said boat owners who get into trouble at sea should have to pay the Coast Guard to be rescued.

NBC didn't think this up, of course. Budget types in Washington have been whining for years about the need for the Coast Guard to charge user fees. Each new high profile rescue effort recharges the old debate over publicly funded rescue at sea. This past spring a seminar at the Naval Academy tackled the issue.

NBC called the findings of its report on Coast Guard rescues a prime example of "The Fleecing of America." A better title would have been "The Wimping of America."

See, this isn't really about money. It's about behavior. In this insulated, cushioned, secure world, going offshore in a sailboat is bad behavior. In a time when wine bottles come with warning labels and restaurants get sued for serving coffee too hot, sailing in harm's way is irresponsible, even reckless, certainly not something to be encouraged by offering free government rescue service.

It costs the Coast Guard about $400 million a year to carry out its search and rescue operations, an amount so small by government spending standards that it doesn't even qualify as a drop in the bucket. It's a drop in the ocean. What's more, it's probably a good guess that the larger part of it is spent on rescuing commercial, not pleasure, craft.

The cost seems out of proportion to the amount of resentment taxpayer-funded rescue at sea generates. The resentment is disappointing because the rescue-at-sea ethic has endured from time immemorial: Seafarers—private, commercial or government sponsored—come to the aid of other seafarers in distress; volunteer lifeboat societies are ingrained in the culture of maritime nations such as England and Ireland; in countries around the world the imperative to help those at the mercy of the cruel sea is honored.

It is, unfortunately, quite easy to deflate the nobility of all of this by observing that much search and rescue effort is spent on saving fools at sea. People who haven't learned how to manage their boats, navigate or understand a weather forecast are remarkably adept at using the radiotelephone to ring up the Coast Guard. Air searches have been initiated by EPIRBs activated by sailors who think seasickness is an emergency. Every year people abandon perfectly good boats in favor of liferafts that, of course, usually don't reach port without a rescue operation.

Saving people from the results of their own foolishness may strike some as a fleecing of taxpayers. On the other hand, making judgments about the worthiness of people for rescue is a playing-God game that the Coast Guard has never fallen for. Long before yachtsmen had EPIRBs the Coast Guard was rescuing seamen from rust bucket freighters and unseaworthy fishing vessels—seafarers who got in trouble through their own negligence.

As a sailing community, our best way to discourage pay-per-rescue nonsense is to encourage proficiency in the central discipline of sailing—self-reliance. The self-reliant sailor possesses in full measure the skills to hand, reef and steer, the knowledge to understand navigation and weather, the humility to know that, in the end, our skills, knowledge and courage might be no match for the sea. For the self-reliant sailor, sending a mayday call is not just a last resort but a painful admission that self-reliance has its limits. Still, we want the option of being able to make that call.

Surprisingly, some self-reliant sailors profess to like the idea of charging a fee for rescue. They argue that it would discourage incompetent boaters from getting into trouble and punish those who do and call the Coast Guard.

Even if that were true, it doesn't change the fact that forcing rescuers to make decisions about who should be rescued is plain wrong. Or that the attitude behind it—that those who have the moxie to sail away from the secure confines of a safety-obsessed society should be prepared to pay for their folly—ought to be offensive to sailors.

This goes to what sailing is. Sailing is more than a chance at intimacy with the sea and the occasional glimpse of a sunset on an uncluttered horizon. A beach cottage or a waterfront condo can provide that without bottom paint and clogged heads.

Sailing is a chance at expanding our lives, of meeting challenges, taking small but invigorating risks, experiencing a whiff of fear while being in charge of our boats and our lives in a vast and uncontrollable environment.

We ought to be able to do that with the knowledge that the age-old ethic of the sea obtains, that seafarers look out for each other. If some of those seafarers happen to be paid by taxpayers, well, it's money well spent in the category of keeping the human spirit healthy.

Even in a Stereo-Size Boat, it's Beautiful Out There

ARE we nuts? A little. It's what makes us so interesting.

I'm referring to sailors. We do some strange things.

Consider Anthony Steward, a South African who recently sailed around the world. The author of the story, who apparently is prone to understatement, uses the words "madman's trip."

Steward set a record—he is the only person to have sailed alone around the world in an open 19-foot dinghy. To one-up him, someone will have to circumnavigate in an 18-foot dinghy or an Optimist pram. Stay tuned. It's bound to happen.

If only he had better documentation, Steward could probably have made other record book entries—like most capsizes during a circumnavigation, most time spent under water during a circumnavigation, most papaws eaten during a circumnavigation.

The first capsize occurred five days out of Cape Town. After that Steward turtled so often he lost count. He reported that the boat was fairly easy to right. Still, he spent a lot of time immersed in various oceans.

That was the easy part. Then came the loss of the rig, keel and rudder, followed by shipwreck on a desert island, where Steward subsisted on papaws. The upside was that papaws are high in beta carotene.

Steward set off on this madman's trip because he was bored with his regular sailing, which included winning the South

African national Finn Class championship. A little nutty? Sure. But also inspirational. This is one brave sailor.

The South African, however, appears positively Rotarian compared to Tom McNally, who sailed across the Atlantic alone. No big deal, you think? Think again. He did it in a boat that was 5'4" long. It took him four and one-half months.

I have information indicating McNally is 50 years old, but nothing about his height. Judging by the photo I'm looking at, I'd say the lanky Englishman is at least six feet tall—and that's after spending 135 days in a boat smaller than some stereo speakers. He was probably 6-6 when he left England.

This was Mr. McNally's third attempt to set the record and, though he claims success, a cloud hangs over it. Gary Speiss feels he still owns the record he set for the smallest boat transatlantic passage some years ago in a comparatively spacious 10-footer because McNally had to be towed in from the Gulf Stream. Maybe they should put McNally in the record book with an asterisk. Both these sailors deserve recognition—in the bold and nutty category.

I met a sailor the other day who, though he won't get his name in any record books, completed a passage that, more than any of the death-defying stunts under sail, made me think about the meaning and mystique of sailing. I found him strolling around the marina. In the course of the conversation we struck up, he told me he had sailed a distance of 140 miles to our harbor in a single non-stop passage that took some 40 hours.

When I raised by eyebrows, he said, "I know it seems like a long time, but my boat is slow and there wasn't much wind and, besides, it was beautiful out there."

This man knows the joys of sailing. It was beautiful out there—why would he want to hurry in?

His words made me feel a twinge of guilt. There was a time

when, if it was beautiful out there, I didn't mind sailing slowly. Simpler times, I guess. Our 30-footer was slow, at least compared to what we expect from a sailboat now, but we loved it. If it took all day to sail 40 miles up the coast, so what? We loved sailing. Getting to where we were going was most of the fun. Years later, when for some perverse reason I have less time for sailing than when I was younger, there are times when I get nervous if our boat's speed under sail falls below what it would make under power. The rattle of the diesel is usually not far behind.

When you fall into that trap it means you're thinking of sailing as transportation, a fool's notion if there ever was one. Almost any conveyance is a more reliable way to get someplace on time.

Sailors spend an inordinate amount of time and money trying to go faster. We're forever tweaking and trimming, buying new stuff, maybe even new boats, to increase our speed of sailing from, say, six knots to six and one-quarter knots. The search for speed under sail, of course, has always been a compelling challenge. That must be why I write so often about boats that defy hull speed or sailors who risk their lives to win races on dangerous overpowered sailing platforms.

Even sailing that is fast is slow compared to virtually any other way to move. That doesn't matter, because the true joys of sailing do not derive from going fast. They come from being there, one with the sea and the wind, in the quiet and purity of nature offshore. Why would we want to shorten that experience, hurry it along?

That's what it's about: We sail because, as the wise sailor said, it's beautiful out there.

PFD-Required Class
Is Not for Sailors

THEY set spinnakers in gales. They sailed at 30 knots, in winds of 50 knots, in seas 40 feet high. They blasted through tunnels of water, were swept by waves that sent sailors fetching up at the end of the safety harness tethers. They broached when a marauding puff of near hurricane-force wind slammed them down or when the helmsman was knocked off the wheel by a wave, and bowmen went aloft in the worst of it to clear away torn sails and fouled halyards. They sailed blind in black, snowy nights, thousands of miles from a safe port but perilously close to icebergs. It was a safety-at-sea advocate's worst nightmare. It was the Whitbread Round the World Race.

A few days after the Whitbread ended and winning skipper Paul Cayard could write, "I am very relieved not to have had to tell anyone's mom or wife or girlfriend that we left them behind," our fleet started the first race of the season. It was a sunny morning and the water, prematurely warmed by hot spring weather, looked like the wavy glass of an old house, its surface barely wrinkled by the 2-knot zephyr.

We all wore life preservers.

The contrast between the daredeviltry of the Whitbread racers and the oh-so-careful way most of the rest of us have to race sailboats in this penultimate year of the millennium suggests that the poles of sailing are mighty far apart. It is interesting that the

Whitbread's outrageous affront to careful seamanship captured what Cayard called the largest audience ever for a sailboat race at a time when a growing element of the boating universe seems obsessed with safety.

We wore PFDs in our race because we had to. It's the rule, the much talked about US Sailing "prescription" that requires PFDs to be worn by everyone on the boat while racing. The intent is noble, and I expect we will soon hear reports of sailors who were saved by flotation they might not have been wearing without the regulation. I try not to be annoyed by how absurd the rule can be in mill pond conditions, and think of it as just one more of many rules of sailboat racing. In that context, abiding by it is a small price to pay for a lot of enjoyment.

Being forced to wear a life jacket at all times on the water, on the other hand, would be too high a price for sailors to pay to enjoy their sport. Yet talk of making PFD wearing mandatory is developing disquieting signs of momentum. In a so-called dialog on the issue presided over by the Coast Guard, considerable support for the requirement has been voiced by law enforcement and boat safety officials and some boat owners.

The rationale for a PFD law is that a certain number of people who fall off of boats drown, and that many of them would survive if they were wearing flotation.

It's true, but it begs the question: What does this have to do with sailing? The answer is ... very little. Boating accident statistics are driven by power boats. Using them to support an argument that sailors, among other boaters, should be forced to wear PFDs is wrong on two counts: Sailing is not an inherently dangerous sport; and sailors are generally well qualified to take care of themselves.

Safety zealots have distorted the majesty of the sea into an unrelenting menace. The real menace, and the cause of most boat accidents, is the incompetence and stupid or reckless behavior of people on boats. There may be something to be said for saving these potential victims from themselves, but, please, not at the expense of the liberty of people who know how to handle themselves on the water.

The latter pretty much describes sailors. Seamanship is inherent in the sailing ethic: to possess the requisite boathandling and navigational skills, to have a knowledge of the sea and the wind, to always respect the seafaring imperative of being prepared and, yes, to know when to use a safety harness and life vest.

This doesn't describe every sailor, of course, but it applies to so many of them that it would be an affront to a whole class of boat owners to strap them into PFDs whether they need them or not.

Picture this: A seasoned skipper and his crew make a competent crossing of the Atlantic in their sturdy 50-foot fiberglass sloop; on their approach to a U.S. port they are accosted by a water cop (probably mounted on a Jet Ski) and cited for failure to wear life jackets.

The popularity of the Round the World Race among sailors, besides validating the fact that, like sex, survival sells, owes something to the vicarious factor. I'm not saying the owner of a Catalina 27 following the Whitbread on the Internet wishes he could be out there dodging icebergs at the 36-knot boat speed one competitor reported, but the adventure is appealing as an extension of our own sailing experiences that test our ability to deal in a seamanlike way with the challenges we encounter at sea.

Hence, the egregiousness of the insult of proposing to put sailors in the PFD-required class—right alongside PWC operators.

It's Not Enough that
Sailing Is Kind to the Environment

COULD it be that, with the electronic eye through which, with such grim fascination, we watch war happen, we have seen the future? We have seen a war fought over oil and, by the monstrous vandal who opened the valves to let crude gush into the Persian Gulf, with oil. Such is oil's pernicious influence on the course of world events that if one day civilization grinds down to a final cosmic battle, Armageddon will probably be a place like the Persian Gulf, where mankind will disappear beneath viscous waves of petroleum like the last dinosaur sucked into the tar pit.

Until then, let's go sailing. But not, please, in the Persian Gulf, even when the mines and warships are gone. The Gulf will probably never be free of its patina of oil. By all accounts, it was an oily mess even before Saddam Hussein committed his outrage, an inevitable consequence of the everyday wounding of the environment by oil trafficking.

Much as we might like to, we can't single out the Middle East for harboring perpetrators of eco-assault by oil. I will never forget the disappointment of our children when we took them, at a young age, to play on a pretty Santa Barbara, California, beach. The sandy shore turned out to be a minefield of glops of oil the consistency of tar washed in from the oil rigs we saw standing in the haze offshore. We had to use paint thinner to clean the kids' feet and hands.

Given all of the gruesome crimes committed upon our oceans on such horrifying scale by big time environmental thugs, it's no surprise that some pleasure boat owners, whose pollution offenses amount to little more than the proverbial mosquito bite on the elephant's behind, are irritated by things like the pollution placard. If your boat is 26 feet or longer, you have been violating federal law since last July 31 if you haven't had one of those displayed aboard.

The plaque, similar to the one about oil that you are required to keep on your boat near the engine, lists items that may not, under the law, be thrown overboard. The same law requires boats 40 feet and longer that have a galley and berths and travel more than three miles offshore to have a waste management plan and a person in charge of it. It also sets penalties of up to $50,000 and five years in jail.

All of this results from a treaty, ratified by a number of nations, designed to control pollution of the seas by commercial vessels. In the U.S. it is interpreted to apply to pleasure craft as well.

Posting signs, generating paperwork, appointing WMOs (waste management officers)—how else would we expect the bureaucracy to protect the environment? If you're irritated by that, you probably also dislike the thought this is yet another way of Big Brother to intrude into one of the last bastions of the unfettered life, a vessel at sea.

On the other hand: As dopey as this approach by government to looking after the earth's water may seem, it is at least an approach. Better this than doing nothing; better a sign that prescribes where it's illegal to dump dunnage (for those of you who haven't served in the Merchant Marine, dunnage is padding used to protect cargo) than to ignore the problem of treating the oceans like garbage cans.

(A legitimate complaint about the plaque is that the rules it specifies are too lenient, allowing the dumping of everything except plastic outside of 25 miles from shore.)

Pleasure boat owners (notice how hard I'm trying, in this day of yacht bashing, to avoid using the suddenly pejorative term "yachtsman") can use a nudge, even a dunderheaded one like this, to waken to environment concern. Fewer sailors than you would expect are in the vanguard of seagoing environmentalists. Recall that it took government restrictions to stop the fouling of inshore waters by overboard-discharge heads and the poisoning of marine life by super-toxic bottom paint.

For a group whose recreation is enhanced so profoundly by clean water, sailors have been surprisingly cavalier in their treatment of the liquid environment. Would that we would all exhibit such tender concern for the sea as the crusty singlehander profiled a while back in *SAILING* who changed his engine oil in mid-ocean and brought every drop of it back to be disposed of on shore. It is more typical that every bit of waste generated on ocean passages goes over the side.

Compared to oil spills and such horrors as hazardous waste disposal in the deep ocean, ocean littering by pleasure boats is small stuff. The callous attitude it represents, however, is offensive. What's more, the littering isn't always small stuff. Racing sailors who are sensitive to the environment are probably still cringing in embarrassment over an incident in a Transpac Race. When one of the fleet-leading ULDBs reached the point on the course where upwind headsails were no longer needed, its crew threw them overboard. The weight-saving expedient was reported to the press after the race by those responsible without so much as a guilty look. This happened before boats were required to carry pollution plaques, but that wouldn't have made a difference. The plaques forbid dumping plastic anywhere in the ocean but say nothing about indestructible Kevlar. Besides, the $50,000 fine wouldn't have been much of a deterrent; the discarded genoas were probably worth almost that much.

Let's consider that an unfortunate aberration. Sailing is gentle on the environment. Sailboats, after all, consume no significant amounts of fuel, contribute no meaningful amounts of smoke or noise to the environment. Yet sailors should not be content with this passive kindness to the environment. It is not enough that we refrain from abusing the water on which we sail. Sailors, of all users of the environment, should be among the most passionate advocates of its protection.

Think of that when you look at the silly sign you had to mount on your boat.

Riddle of the
Linda E.

A STONE'S *throw from my office, a fishing vessel leaves its mooring in front of a sagging fish shanty around 5 a.m. Often it doesn't return until 5 p.m. This happens every day, even in the dead of winter. It happens when it's 20 below zero, when a snowstorm is raging, when the lake is in the throes of a roaring northeaster.*

Now, it doesn't happen any more, and that is both a sad story and a cautionary tale for sailors.

I wrote the italicized words several years ago about a boat named *Linda E.* in a column about the hard lot of those who, unlike us recreational sailors, go to sea not for the fun of it, but because they have to, in fair weather or foul, to make a living.

For 60 years, fishermen made a living on the *Linda E.* The 42-foot steel-hulled gill-netter took them far out into Lake Michigan and, even in the gales of winters, always brought them back. Until December 11, 1998, when the *Linda E.* disappeared with her crew of three.

The boat's disappearance was complete, perfect in a terrible way. There was no distress signal, not so much as a fragment of wreckage, not a trace. It was a mystery then, and as this is written one year later, it is still a mystery that tortures the families of the lost fishermen and, in a different way, tortures the U.S. Coast Guard.

As if to underscore the fickleness of fate, this survivor of the brutal weather of so many winters disappeared on an uncharacteristically benign day on Lake Michigan—cloudless, a light southerly breeze, a small swell. The boat left its berth in Port Washington, Wisconsin, before sunrise. Later, from a location only nine miles from port, a crewman used a cellular telephone to call the the local fish processing house to report a good catch of half a ton of chubs. These were the last words ever heard from the *Linda E.*

The search began at sunset. Ships and planes and commercial fishing boats, even shore parties combing beaches for wreckage, searched for days, and found nothing.

Seafaring mysteries don't get much more baffling than this one. Something happened to a sound, seaworthy vessel with such shocking suddenness that there were not even a few seconds of grace for a distress call by cell phone or VHF radio, no time to put on PFDs and abandon ship. The lack of debris ruled out an explosion. The sterling reputation of 61-year-old Capt. Leif Weborg for personal integrity and professional competence all but ruled out theories of skulduggery and negligence.

A wreath with a yellow ribbon was hung on a piling at the *Linda E.'s* vacant dock, and families of the lost fishermen, knowing, but of course not really knowing, they would never see them again, began grieving. Meanwhile, the Coast Guard began its investigation, not knowing that it was headed for a maritime disaster of its own.

The agency gave no information to the public or the families. Commercial fishermen, though, didn't need to hear from the Coast Guard. In fact, they had a message for the investigators: The *Linda E.* had surely been run down by a freighter, tanker or barge.

Coast Guard spokesmen downplayed—disingenuously, it turned out—the possibility of a collision, but others saw the logic of it, and a way to prove it—find and raise the *Linda E.* From the position of its nets, searchers would have a general idea where to look. High-tech sonar imaging equipment had discovered wrecks in more challenging circumstances. "Raise the Linda E.!" became a rallying cry among the families and fishermen. The Coast Guard's response was a terse disclaimer: We don't do salvage operations.

Two developments turned up the heat on the agency. The first was the crash of John F. Kennedy Jr.'s airplane off the coast of New England. As in the *Linda E.*, three lives were lost and the wreckage lay on the bottom of the sea. The Coast Guard, with the help of the Navy, found and raised the plane and the bodies of its passengers, but continued to refuse to do the same for the fishing boat and its passengers. Friends of the *Linda E.* decried the double standard.

If the Coast Guard was feeling the pressure, it didn't show it. Though its investigation was complete, it withheld its report in spite of the pleas of the *Linda E.* families. Then the other shoe dropped. A newspaper obtained a copy of the report and published its findings. This produced an uproar, because it revealed that the Coast Guard had circumstantial evidence early on that the boat was run down and sunk by a tanker-barge.

(Some disclosure here: The journalist who acquired the report and broke the story is Bill Schanen IV, my son and managing editor of *Ozaukee Press* in Port Washington, Wisconsin.)

The blockbuster in the report is the fact that within days of the disappearance Coast Guard investigators learned that a 454-foot, 5,000-ton tanker-barge pushed by a tug had been steaming on a course that took it over the position of the fishing vessel's nets on the day it disappeared. Traces of white paint—the *Linda E.* was painted white—were found on the tanker's bow.

Since the collision evidence became public knowledge, "Raise the Linda E.!" has become a chorus, and some of the singers are members of Congress, who, harsh in their criticism of the Coast Guard, are demanding that the fishing boat be found and raised. To which the agency has responded that its investigation is closed.

Well, I said it was a sad story, sad as a human tragedy and as a revealing look at an unresponsive, insensitive government agency at work.

The issue, of course, is not salvage; it's evidence. The wreck of the *Linda E.* could well contain not only the bodies of three fishermen but the story of how they met their deaths, evidence of a maritime crime of negligence and a deadly threat to safety at sea. If that isn't the Coast Guard's business, what is?

As for the cautionary aspect of the tale, imagine how the *Linda E.* may have met its end—in a collision of such explosive force that the smaller vessel was rolled, holed and sunk in an instant, so suddenly that everything on board was carried to the bottom with it. The crew of the barge, of course, would not have been looking, either out of the tug windows nearly 500 feet behind its high bow or at the radar screen.

The lesson for sailors is obvious but bears stating: Never assume that the ship sees you.

When I first wrote about the *Linda E.* it was just a doughty, old fishing boat, little known outside of its home port. Now its name rings in the halls of Congress and it has achieved an accidental fame—for the mystery and tragedy associated with it, and for the strange way its disappearance was handled by the U.S. Coast Guard.

How the *Linda E.* was Found

THEY found the fishing boat where common sense said it would be, near where it had last set its nets, on the bottom of Lake Michigan, under 260 feet of water. The U.S. Navy minesweeper *Defender* spent a Sunday examining the lake bottom with its mine-detecting sonar, discovered a likely wreck and sent down a remote-controlled, video-equipped vehicle that transmitted the image for which so many had waited so long—a weathered hull bearing the letters *Linda E.* It was so easy, certainly the easiest accomplishment in the strange history of the tragedy I first wrote about in a column entitled "Riddle of the *Linda E.*"

The riddle was: How could a seaworthy 42-foot steel-hulled fishing boat disappear from the face of the lake in calm weather without a trace? On December 11, 1998, from a position nine miles offshore, a crewmember called the local fish processing house to report that the boat was returning to port with a catch of half a ton of chubs. Nothing was ever heard again from the *Linda E.* Three men were lost with the boat.

The Coast Guard began an investigation, but ruled out searching for the presumably sunken vessel.

The Coast Guard didn't find the *Linda E.*, but owing to its strange handling of its investigation, it did find a storm of frustration and anger, not just on the part of the families of the lost fishermen and the commercial fishing community, but among recreational boaters, including the many sailors who wrote me after the column appeared, and finally among the public and even members of Congress.

This was the inevitable result of the agency's obdurate refusal to search the lake bottom, using available private or government sources, and its decision to keep its report secret long after its investigation was completed. When a newspaper obtained a copy and published the report's findings, the public relations disaster was complete. The report revealed that the Coast Guard had circumstantial evidence within days of the boat's disappearance that the *Linda E.* could have been run down by a 454-foot, 5,000-ton tanker barge that had steamed over the position of the fishing vessel's nets on the day it disappeared. No matter, the investigation was closed, the Coast Guard said.

Now, eight months later, the *Linda E.* has been found, and the investigation is no longer closed. Here's how it happened:

The Coast Guard gave up on the *Linda E.*, but many individuals didn't. One of them was Mark Green, member of the House of Representatives from Green Bay, Wisconsin. Green's is a refreshing story of a congressman taking up the cause of not the usual powerful special interest group, but one of the least influential groups of constituents imaginable—a few families of the economically distressed and fast declining commercial fishing community.

The freshman congressman, perhaps naively, went to the Coast Guard with the expectation that members of Congress (he enlisted other representatives and senators in the cause) might get results where ordinary citizens could not. No less than the commandant of the Coast Guard told Green what the agency had told everyone else: It's not our job.

In the end, help was found not in Washington but in the fishing and shipbuilding town of Marinette, Wisconsin, where Sandy

Saunier read a newspaper story about the Navy's plans to have two minesweepers cruise Lake Michigan on a training and recruiting mission. Saunier, owner of the Marine Bar and Grill in Marinette, had lost a father, a brother and a nephew to commercial fishing accidents on the lake. The nephew was aboard the *Linda E.* Saunier knew one of the minesweepers, the 224-foot *Defender*, well; it had been built in Marinette and she had attended its launching. She knew it had equipment that could find the *Linda E.* She suggested to Green, why not use it as part of the training exercise?

Why not, indeed. Green got Adm. Joe Betancourt, commander of the Mine Warfare Command, to agree to let the *Defender* and the other minesweeper scan the bottom in the area of the *Linda E.*'s nets.

After that, as I said, it was easy. The *Defender* found the *Linda E.* near the position of its nets—and near the course of the tanker barge as recorded by waypoints in its log.

The discovery forced the reopening of an investigation that should never have been closed. It was heartening to see the Coast Guard react at once by dispatching the buoy tender *Acacia* to inspect the wreck with high-resolution video cameras and, it turned out, to document extensive damage. But then it announced—again—that it will not raise the *Linda E.*

Perhaps someone else will. The best evidence of what caused the deaths at sea of three men, evidence perhaps of shipping negligence that could threaten recreational and commercial boat operators, is within reach. The divers and equipment needed to raise the vessel, even from its fairly daunting depth, are available. The riddle of the *Linda E.* may yet be solved. Though probably not by the Coast Guard.

To some people, the agency that had come across as stubborn and insensitive now seems obtuse as well. They ask, If a fisherman's aunt can come up with the idea of using a high-tech Navy vessel on a training mission to search for the *Linda E.*, why couldn't the Coast Guard?

Coast Guard spokesmen have blamed budget constraints for the "it's not our job" attitude. They have a point. The agency is not adequately funded for all it is expected to do, and this surely is an egregious sin of government at a time when the federal budget surplus is predicted to be $1.9 trillion.

Yet sometimes the Coast Guard seems to be its own worst enemy. It lost friends with its handling of the sinking of a fishing vessel, even among those of us who think of it as a noble protector of seafarers, even in the Congress that controls its funding.

On Sailboats

The Boat that
Changed Everything

WHEN the selection committee of the American Sailboat Hall of Fame considered boats for induction this year, one boat was an instant consensus pick. No question, no argument, no doubt. No wonder—it was the Cal 40, the boat that changed everything.

When I assigned a young staff member to write a profile of the Cal 40 and told him that when it was introduced in 1963 it was considered a radical and possibly dangerous racing design, he gave me one of those "jeez, he's lost it" looks. I couldn't blame him. The Cal 40 doesn't have the predatory look of today's ocean racers, no angles, sharp edges or towering fractional rig. But, make no mistake, it was a predator, one that preyed on conventional thinking.

The Cal 40's gently dipping sheerline, curved, spoon-bow, counter stern and squatty sailplan gave it a deceptively soft appearance. But there was nothing soft below the waterline. In an era of wineglass-shaped hulls with deep, slack bilges, the Cal 40 had a shallow dinghy-like hull with firm cheeks. The keel was a fin.The rudder—gasp!—was not attached to the keel, and this was heresy.

Conventional wisdom made the rudder a hinged extension of the keel. On the Cal 40 it was a freestanding spade at the end of the waterline. What it did back there was to give the helmsman exquisite control of the boat, particularly in fast off-wind sailing.

Perhaps the reason it had not appeared earlier on big boats was that offshore boats of the time were rarely in danger of going fast enough to need a spade rudder.

The Cal 40 needed it. While other displacement boats were at the mercy of the law of hull speed, the Cal 40 thumbed its nose at it. The shape of the hull and its appendages combined with relatively light weight gave the boat the ability to get up on the waves and surf. Sailing a 40-foot boat had never been so thrilling.

Just how thrilling was evident in a photo that appeared on the cover of a new magazine called *SAILING* in 1969. Our covers weren't glossy then; they weren't even printed in color. But that cover, featuring the Cal 40 *Melee*, is still one of my favorites. The boat, embraced in great plumes of pure white spray, is locked onto an enormous wave, surfing to the finish of the Miami-Nassau race. Though the wind is so strong the boat is carrying a poled-out genoa instead of a spinnaker, the three visible crew members look nonchalant as they enjoy the ride of their lives on a boat that is in perfect control.

Sailors like to cultivate a swashbuckling image, but as an establishment they tend to be conservative. And so when the Cal 40 appeared, it was ridiculed as some sort of wacky California take on sailboat design and criticized as unseaworthy. The rudder would break off; the keel would drop off; the hull would fail.

None of that happened; there was no chance of it happening. The Cal 40 was a carefully engineered, strongly built fiberglass yacht. It was only somewhat lighter than other 40-footers, but the difference was accentuated by its long waterline, which yielded a displacement/length ratio of 250 at a time when the norm was more like 330.

The boat was thought of as a downwind machine, but in fact it was an all-around boat, fast on any point of sail. The best indication of that is that Cal 40s won both the Transpac Race, mostly a surfing contest, and the Bermuda race, usually an upwind slog. In the 1996 Bermuda Race, five of the first 15 places overall were won by Cal 40s. Cal 40s won three consecutive Transpacs in 1965, '66 and '67. Incredibly, 22 years after it was designed, a Cal 40 won the 1985 Transpac.

No production boat has ever dominated racing the way the Cal 40 did, yet it would be wrong to classify it as a pure racer. Classify it instead as, simply, a good boat. Long after its racing heyday, the Cal 40 delights its owners as a safe, comfortable, easy-to-handle offshore cruising boat.

The Cal 40 was not chosen for the Hall of Fame because of its racing record. It was chosen because it propelled big-boat sailing to the future. Sailboat design was progressing in microscopic increments until the Cal 40 took it on a great leap forward. It leapt so far that today's fastest racing boats are refined Cal 40s with fin keels, spade rudders and shallow hulls free of rule induced distortions. They are far more sophisticated in many ways than the Cal 40, but you could say that, essentially, they were designed 33 years ago.

The designer of the Cal 40 is Bill Lapworth. His creation now has a place in the American Sailboat Hall of Fame and he, retired and living in Virginia, has, in the minds of knowing sailors at least, a place in the pantheon of the world's most influential sailboat designers. There are some revered names in that group, but Lapworth may be the only one about whom it can be said—he changed everything.

Annals of the Self-Reliant Sailor

ONE of the most important improvements in sailing in the last decade is high-tech rope: braided fibers stronger than steel, looking cool in their gaudy covers, with names that sound like the Millennium Falcon's ports of call—Vizzion, Aracom, Spectron, Vectrus. I love the stuff.

But, then, I love low-tech rope too, good old three-strand nylon. There's almost no reason to use it these days, with the arguable exception of the anchor rode. But I keep some around, for the ostensible purpose of making up dock lines (you can never have too many, right?) or short lengths of line that, who knows, might be needed someday to secure something somewhere. The real purpose of this rope, of course, is to give me something to splice. Because a sailor should splice rope.

To gently unlay the strands and then, fingers working with their own memory of an oft-repeated task, to weave, pull and tuck the strands to create a well-made eye splice or to join lines with an elegantly slim long splice is a satisfying sailor's ritual.

I am afraid I can't say the same about splicing high-tech braided line. For me, this is a chore akin to assembling the gas grill that comes home in a deceptively small box—something to be done by the numbers. No matter how many times I do it, I need to study drawings and step-by-step instructions before I set to the challenge with tape, marker, ruler, fid and one of those epée-like fid pushers. It's all too complex to be a satisfying hands-on exercise. Moreover, unlike my handsome three-strand splices, the results are rarely pretty. Suffice it to say, I can splice exotic rope if I have to.

That isn't saying much, but at least it meets the ancient standard of sailing: A sailor is self-reliant. Our boats can take us far from the safety net of conveniences that keeps our lives on shore secure. So we learn to take care of ourselves on boats.

We figure out how to make the splice, tie the right knot, service the winch, stop leaks in hatches, portholes, deck and hull, get aloft to untangle halyards, steer the boat when the rudder breaks, fix the head.

The truth is, of course, most of us don't sail far enough away to *have* to do these things. We do them because, odd as it may sound, we like to. (I'm exempting head repair from this part of the discussion.) It's about the satisfaction of knowing we're able to do what it takes to manage our boats.

I have a vivid memory of the "we can do it" ethic of good sailors from a time when our boat went down hard in a violent broach 150 miles from the finish of an offshore race. After the requisite time on her beam ends (which seemed like hours but was probably only seconds) the boat staggered upright, spinnaker still flogging, shaking off water like a retriever. It looked as though we had escaped unscathed ... until the boom emerged from the water deeply kinked at the attachment point of the vang. In the 30-knot breeze, it was a foregone conclusion that the boom would break if we didn't drop the mainsail (which would have taken us out of the race) or devise a jury rig in a hurry.

Led with alacrity by our most devoted exponent of marlinspike seamanship, the crew pillaged the boat for splints, scavenging a guard rail from the galley and a long stainless steel handhold from the head. These were lashed to the damaged boom with small-diameter (high-tech, of course) line and then the whole affair was wrapped with line until it looked like a whipping on a giant piece of rope. The reinforced boom, though still kinked enough to give the mainsail the sort of elephant's-behind look you see on a badly trimmed spinnaker, held through hours of heavy weather and was still strong at the finish.

I still find it interesting that in a record-setting race remembered for its sailing thrills, the high point was a near disaster. An aerial photo of the boat running at speed with a bent, splinted and seized boom remains a cherished memento of self-reliant sailing.

I can empathize with those who lament the decline of hands-on navigation in this day of gadgets that produce instant and near-perfect fixes, compute our courses and plan our routes—do seemingly everything short of making dinner reservations.

These gadgets now are so good (not to mention so cheap that we can have backups for our backup GPSs) that sailors who aren't interested in learning about dead reckoning and plotting courses on charts can get along fine. But they deprive themselves of some of the satisfaction that comes with being a self-reliant sailor.

Charts play a role in that, sort of like that three-strand splice that doesn't serve much purpose beyond making the splicer feel salty. I keep a collection of full-size government charts aboard, even though it has been years since I really needed them. Carefully unfolding them (there are chart rollers and chart folders; I'm a folder and proud of it), laying off courses and marking positions is like tucking those strands in a splice—a rewarding sailor's ritual.

Charts are enjoyable companions too in that the navigator's hieroglyphics they bear from years of use are a penciled history of sailing experiences, of passages cruising and racing. If I work at it, I can find the circled dot beside the time of day written as 1118 at a point a mile and a half off Sleeping Bear Point. It was the position I recorded a few seconds before the broach that almost broke the boom and gave a crew a chance to prove they were self-reliant sailors.

Heeling is a Drag—
in More Ways than One

ONE of my first sailing memories is of being assured, at a barely post-toddler age, that I shouldn't worry, the boat would lean over, but it wouldn't tip over. I took it to heart. Heeling became an old friend. For years I also invested blind faith in my mentor's optimistic appraisal of the stability of keelboats. I was to learn that, of course, everything capsizes. Now I am wondering about heeling.

To any (monohull) sailor who's been at it for a while, sailing on an angle is as natural as sleeping horizontally. Heeling, to a degree, seems right. There is a moment, just after a tack when the wind fills the sails from the new side and the boat leans smoothly to that magic angle that signals the acquisition of the groove, when heeling tells the helmsman all is right with the world, or at least with his boat.

But that is not what heeling tells first-time sailors. What it tells them is that something is wrong. Tipping goes contrary to instinct. No other form of recreational conveyance that comes to mind decides to tilt on its own. Skiers and cyclists may heel, but they do it at their discretion. Airplanes heel only when their pilots tell them to. There are people in the sailing industry, which has long been in the throes of a navel-gazing exercise aimed at figuring out why new sailors aren't hopping on board faster, who say heeling is the culprit.

Heeling surely is the culprit in making most monohull sail-boats models of inefficiency in achieving forward motion. Most designs benefit from a small degree of heel. Beyond that, heeling is all bad. You can judge how bad by the lengths designers and owners go to counteract it. A modern racing boat will have more than half of its weight in a deep lead ballast bulb. This produces the ability to carry a large expanse of sail—and a jerky ride not unlike that provided by an unbroken horse of nasty disposition. And still the owner is required to add the weight of 12 bodies on the rail of his 40-foot boat to be competitive.

These boats are exciting to sail, and in their construction techniques and materials are elegant exemplars of the best of high-tech. But they are also smoking guns on the evidence trail that suggest that in some ways sailing is still firmly anchored in the past. Here we are at the millennium still piling on weight to make our boats stand up. You could make the case that we did that better a century ago by ballasting sailing canoes with crew weight efficiently perched on hiking boards or with sandbags on deck (which could at least be tossed overboard for the downwind leg).

There are better ideas, but it has been hard to get them into the mainstream of sailing. Some of them can be found in Shock 40, a production boat that uses a canting ballast bulb to keep heeling to a salutary 10 degrees or so. The idea, if not the necessarily the apparatus to make it work, is simple: Cock the bulb to weather and it becomes a far more efficient counter to the pressure of the sails. To replace the keel's lost anti-leeway effect, add two deep foils called canards that will also steer the boat. The idea has been around for a quite a while at an esoteric level. Now it's available as an off-the-shelf heeling remedy.

A friend said this about sailing with canting ballast and the pleasing effect of minimizing heeling: "My wife, who would rather be in a burning building than on a heeling boat, could sit on the same side all day, adjust the heel to her desire at the to touch of a button. "

Multihull sailors, of course, would ask, Why bother? Who needs the complexity of an adjustable ballast bulb? In fact, who needs ballast? If you want to sail flat, sail boats with two or three hulls. The soaring popularity of catamarans and trimarans suggests that a growing number of people believe this is the way we were meant to sail—on top of the water, making no hole in the sea, dragging no lead.

Detractors can recite the standard drawbacks—multihulls are still not very handy sailing upwind or navigating a marina and they can tip over (but, then, everything capsizes). But they don't heel.

While on the subject of multihulls, I should mention that I have firsthand knowledge of one situation in which heeling mono-hulls have an advantage over flat-riding multis. This is when they are aground. Once in remote area of the Florida Keys while I was engaged in an activity that enthusiasts might describe as extreme gunkholing, I put a large cruising two-huller firmly on the bottom in an ebbing tide. (No mean trick in itself, since the boat's draft was all of 30 inches.) In a monohull, we would have trimmed the sails, heeled hard and sailed off the putty. The cat, of course, just sat there, solid on her two hulls, like a monument to my eyeball navigation hubris.

That aside, there's more bad than good to say about heeling. The fact that heeling turns off new sailors may mean they are smarter about the sport than old sailors. Heeling is indeed a drag—in more ways than one.

A final thought: The sailboats that are the fastest in the world—tri-foilers—do not heel.

Life Without Genoas—
What a Concept

A revolution is afoot. Radicals have taken over sailboat rig design. New offshore boats are appearing with nonoverlapping headsails. Yes, without genoas.

Only in sailing, where the past is often the future, could a concept this old be considered revolutionary.

It is of some concern that we have sailed for so long and are still not sure of what is the most effective way to arrange our sails. But let's be thankful for small favors. If the return of the nonoverlapping jib and the realization that the mainsail really is the *main* sail mean the death of the genoa, I say … rest in peace.

That's not something I would have said earlier in my sailing life, the formative years of which were spent in the Golden Age of the Genoa. In that epoch, it was dogma that boat speed was directly related to the distance that the headsail overlapped the mast. This was expressed as a percentage of the base of the foretriangle. Many sailors of the time could proudly say, much as a sports car buff boasts of the horsepower under his Porsche's hood, that they sailed with a 170. On most boats a 170 percent genoa overlaps the cockpit.

On two halcyon days last spring in the haze-filtered sunshine and ample sea breeze off Newport, Rhode Island, I experienced a headsail epiphany. In the New York Yacht Club Spring Regatta, I sailed as the headsail trimmer on a boat that did not have a genoa. I can best describe the experience as relaxing. Feeling like the Maytag repairman, I mainly watched the jib tack itself.

Though an old idea, the fractional 100 percent jib on this boat benefitted from a new wrinkle, a patented Jib Boom that made the headsail perfectly self-tacking and kept its shape efficient when sheets were eased for a reach or run.

For Garry Hoyt, inventor of the device and our helmsman, the regatta was validation of his low opinion of the genoa. It was hard to tell whether he derived more pleasure from beating most of the boats in our class or from watching the populous crews of the conventional masthead racer-cruisers wrestle with their monster genoas. Our crew, incidentally, numbered a sedate three.

Hoyt's Alerion 38 yawl made its statement on the obsolescence of the genoa as a cruising boat, but it is on Grand Prix racing boats where the nonoverlapping jibs have most dramatically rewritten the conventional wisdom. This year's racing phenoms have been the Corel 45 and Farr 40, Bruce Farr designs that are winning races with astonishing regularity but without genoas. On their debuts, they were, predictably, greeted with skepticism. Probably will work in heavy air, the naysayers allowed, but they'll be dogs when the breeze is light.

Well, the overlappers were only half wrong. The genoaless boats have proved fast in all conditions. Their enormous mainsails are powerful engines, effectively complemented by tall, short-footed jibs that work without any of the overlap we were told was essential in upwind performance.

The success of these boats has accelerated a return to headsail sanity that started some time ago. Foretriangles have been getting smaller, as have genoa overlaps, since the day when genoas were worshiped as virtually the sole source of a boat's sail power. It may be significant that this was about the same time that polyester bellbottoms were the rage.

During this period mainsails atrophied into a shape described as "high aspect." This didn't mean that the sail was tall but that the boom was ridiculously short. Zealots of the incredible shrinking mainsail school proclaimed that the sole purpose of the sail was to serve as a vane to balance the helm and create a slot for that wondrous genoa.

Before we bury the genoa, let us praise it for what it can do. Sheeted for a beat, the modern racing genoa, particularly when built with the high-tech materials and techniques available to today's sailmakers, is a beautifully functional foil. If we never had to change tacks or sail off the wind, we wouldn't be burying it.

But we have to do those things, and then the genoa's warts become obvious. They are brutish things to pull around the mast during tacks, taxing equipment and crew, shortening the life of the sail and spoiling the tacking maneuver. Eased off, they lose their reason for existence. Overlap then is not just useless, it robs performance by backwinding the main. Reaching in a seaway, the deck-sweeping sails collect water on the foredeck. Back in the days of polyester bellbottoms, genoas were equipped with an eye in the foot into which a halyard could be shackled to hoist the bottom of the sail off the deck, which merely succeeded in creating a bathtub for really big waves to fill.

If a genoa ever made sense, it was as a specialized racing sail. It's odd, then, that wrapped up on the furlers of so many cruising boats are big genoas, upwind racing sails on boats that rarely race and rarely go upwind. Chalk it up as another example of how cruising design often follows racing ideas to little good effect. But that's changing too. More new cruising designs show up every year sans genoa.

For their part, one-design sailors must be amused by the startling revelation that sailing with big mainsails and small jibs is better. They've been sailing that way forever.

Watching a red Corel 45 lay waste to an IMS racing fleet last summer, I remarked to a friend that the boat's combination of a powerful mainsail and a nonoverlapping jib represented a significant step forward for sailing.

"Yeah," he replied, "that's what they said about the Star boat when it was introduced in 1911."

We Love Our Compass, Heart and Sole

THE Danforth lunch hook carelessly deposited in a cockpit locker. The forgotten screwdriver in the helmsman's pocket. We've all heard about, or committed, these compass sins.

My favorite compass error story, though, comes from a reader in Charlevoix, Michigan. I'll let Roy Herald tell it:

"It has been slightly over six months since my loss of the George LaBlance Memorial Race and I can now speak somewhat rationally about what happened to me while racing across Lake Michigan from Beaver Island to Charlevoix in the fog. I like to sit on the port coaming with my leg crossed over my knee facing my compass in weather conditions like this. Little did I realize that the metal plate in my new Sperry Top-Siders was affecting the accuracy of my compass. We were at one point far ahead of our fleet, assuring us of a first place. The fog cleared as we approached the finish and to our horror found ourselves four miles off course. Instead of our coveted first place, we came in fourth. Shame on the maker of these shoes for not at least putting a warning in serious sailor shoes."

Who'd have thought it—the steel shanks in boat shoes operating as an alien magnetic force inducing compass error? Chalk it up as a reminder that the compass is not foolproof. But that's no fault of the magnetic compass, which is nothing less than the most nearly perfect, the most reliable and the most indispensible instrument sailors use, even though it is by far the oldest.

Hard to believe that a descendant of the device the Vikings used 1,000 years ago to guide them on their epic voyages is the heart of the some of the most sophisticated systems on today's vessels. Autopilots and sailing performance instruments rely on fluxgate compasses that are really not that far removed from the Viking "compass," which was likely a piece of iron ore called lodestone floating on a chip in a bowl of water. They both function by reacting to the magnetic pull emanating from the general area of the North Pole.

Mostly, of course, today's compasses are used in the same way the Vikings used theirs—simply to steer a course. The modern magnetic compass, with bowl, gimbaled card and dome, is an exquisite instrument elegantly adapted for that purpose. And because, unlike the vulnerable electronic gizmos many of us sail with (including fluxgate compasses with digital read-outs), the traditional compasses require no power source other than that great magnet in the core of the planet, it always works when you need it.

Electronic devices haven't replaced the compass, but they do support it in rather convenient ways. With GPS on board to instantly monitor the effect of compass error, it's easy to correct the bearing along the way. Our correspondent with ferrous metal in his boat shoes would be polishing his trophy now if he had a GPS on board.

Still, the compass is such a jewel of an instrument that it is a shame not to have it perfectly adjusted. That includes, of course, compiling a deviation table, which, as you all know (if not, refer to your **Chapman's** at once), records magnetic influences inherent in the boat that drag the compass needle off its proper alignment.

And then, don't forget that the variation for the location in which you are sailing (the difference between magnetic north and geographic north) must be applied. You can try to figure out "compass least, error east; compass best, error west," a hoary navigator's saw that has probably confused more people than it's helped, or let your GPS give you the course with the variation factored in.

No amount of adjustment or care in calculating deviation and variation, however, can make up for human error, the most common form of compass error. Steering by compass, given the leeway caused by current and wind, the difficulty of holding a course in heavy seas and the brain's limited ability to concentrate, is hardly an exercise in precision. Which is what makes dead reckoning navigation such an adventure and is why we have lighthouses and charts that identify stacks, water towers and fuel tanks.

Certainly we should try to live up to our compass' high standard, for if an inanimate object can be a sailor's friend, then the compass surely is that. For the helmsman on a bracing night watch, when the breeze and seas are up and the stars and moon are covered by the low sky, the compass card rocking sedately in its oil-filled hemisphere, bathed in warm pink light, is a trusted and comforting cockpit companion.

That thought reminds me that there is a small chink in the compass' armor. Though the compass never fails, its frail 12-volt light inevitably does so. Here, then, is my compass tip of the month: Keep some chemical light sticks aboard. When the compass light goes out, activate a light stick and duct-tape it to the compass dome. The chartreuse-colored ones I've used are as easy on the helmsman's eyes as pink, and they last through a night.

And one more piece of compass advice—watch where you put your feet.

The 'Jump In' Boats

I have been lucky enough to own some of the boats I've lusted after, but not my first love. I did get to sail her, though, and I can still feel the thrill.

She was a Dyer Dink sailing dinghy. The boat is built today in a similar design—same perky sheer, resolute bow and shapely transom—but it's not the same because it's fiberglass. The boat I loved was built when the idea of mass producing plastic boats was but a gleam in some genius's eye, and my age could still be expressed in a single digit.

The 10-foot boat was built of wood, lapstrake style. I'll never forget her color. Her mahogany planks were almost blond, a warm palomino glowing through a perfect patina of varnish. The Dink was maintained to such a high level on the Bristol fashion meter that the fasteners and fittings always looked the color of freshly cast bronze.

The older boy who owned her hung out, as I did, at the yacht club while his father and my parents were out racing their Star boats. One day as I watched him—forlornly, I suppose—sail the dinghy around the harbor, he brought the boat expertly to the dock, and said to me, "Jump in."

Flustered by the opportunity to at last sail in the object of my desire, I stuttered, "Really?"

"Yeah, really. Jump in!"

The boat floated a good four feet below the dock, and I was no lightweight; it would be understating the case to say I was a stout lad. I jumped.

Thanks to either the skill of the Dyer shipwrights or a miracle of physics, I didn't plunge through those gorgeous blond lapstrakes, but the poor boat did everything but turtle at the dock.

Looking as though he deeply regretted his invitation, the boy began bailing the water that came aboard as a result of my free fall, and said, "Listen, when someone says jump in a boat, you don't just jump in."

My new friend meant only to pass on good advice, not to turn me off of sailing, and I learned not only how to get into small boats, but how to sail them, in many happy hours spent in that beautiful dinghy.

Lucky me. Others who have tried to approach sailing have been told—if not in so many words, then in the daunting nature of the equipment, conventions and institutions of sailing—that you can't jump in. Sailing is too complex, expensive and even dangerous to just jump into it.

Even in sailing, thank goodness, things change. The change to a welcoming attitude has been evolutionary. The change in equipment came later but is more dramatic. What is happening now in entry-level sailboats is nothing less than a full-scale revolution. People with a yen for sailing now have a choice of boats that fairly shout, "C'mon, jump in!"

Three that make that invitation irresistible are the Hobie Wave, the WindRider and the Escape.

The Wave wraps the traditional advantages of a catamaran—stability, beachability and exciting performance into a 13-foot-long package consisting of two unsinkable, indestructible hulls, a pair of rudders that automatically kick up and a simple rig with a Windsurfer-type sail. The boat can be transported on the top of a car, set up in a few minutes and sailed by anyone. It's so easy to sail that even a novice can singlehand it. But with the space provided by its vinyl trampoline, it can just as easily be sailed by a crowd.

The WindRider is an exotic looking trimaran bristling with new ideas—you steer with your feet in an airplane-style cockpit—but so simple to operate that a rank beginner can figure it out in a few minutes. Its beginner-friendliness is aided by that great gift of multihulls, stability that instills confidence without inhibiting performance.

The WindRider is a one-person boat, and the Escape, too, is set up to be sailed solo, though it can carry two adults. It's an 11-foot, 6-inch dinghy built of new ideas—a hull shape that virtually defies heeling and capsizing, a rotating boom that keeps the rig simple and the sail fully efficient off the wind and on; and an incredibly clever trimming dial that works with a wind indicator and the color-coded sheet to act as a mechanical sailing instructor. Beyond simplicity, the thrust of the design is to eliminate the tippy feeling that turns off so many first-time sailors. The hull of the Escape is so stable that I'm pretty sure a stout lad could cannonball it from a high dock without bringing a drop of water aboard.

These boats, all three of which are built of roto-molded polyethylene, are remarkable in that they have created simplicity out of high-tech, but where they differ most from foregoing entry-level boats is that they've managed to keep all of the fun in sailing. I've heard from longtime, sophisticated sailors who love sailing these beginner boats.

Their greatest charm, though, is that these boats say: Jump in, no experience necessary, no sailing lessons needed. Nonsailors can teach themselves to sail these boats, or learn from a friend. Formal sailing instruction can come later to, as in skiing, perfect technique and move to the next level.

Meanwhile, thanks to the "jump in" boats, the first level of sailing is more rewarding than ever, even the days of exquisite, varnished sailing dinghies.

Tin Men Don't Do
Bottoms Anymore

ONCE I dreamed of being a professional sailor. I had this dream so long ago that professional sailors as we know them today, rich sailing celebrities like Dennis Conner and Paul Cayard, had not been invented. Professional sailors then were guys hired by owners to take care of their boats. Owners sometimes burnished the status of having such employees by calling them their captains.

I couldn't imagine a more glamorous life. Being paid to sail was only part of its appeal. The rest of it was the image. The thought of being in charge of a magnificent racing yacht, of making triumphant harbor entrances while issuing crisp orders from the helm, of recruiting crews and entertaining handsome women attracted to the handsome boat and its handsome captain, of winning races for a grateful and generous owner, was irresistible.

One winter in my high school years I sought out a locally famous captain to hear some sailing stories to feed my dreams of a career as a sailing professional. I found him in a boatyard shed at the end of a day. I heard his cough before I made him out in the murky light, through clouds of suspended paint dust. Up close he looked like a rusty Tin Man.

Grinding away with a power sander, he had for days been stripping thick bottom paint, brown stuff full of poisonous metals and noxious chemicals, from the wooden hull of the big ocean racer he was paid to care for. His clothes, once the faded "tans" that were the uniform of the boat professionals of the day, had been dyed umber by airborne pigment. His face had a metallic sheen; the pores of the skin of his hands were clogged with grit. Dark red powder was layered under his fingernails, in his ears and nostrils; his eyes were red with irritation. I saw no sign of goggles or a breathing mask. What I saw was a side of a paid sailor's life that was so far from glamorous that it persuaded me to rethink my career plans.

Needless to say, I never became a professional sailor. That didn't save me, though, from looking much like my erstwhile idol some years later. Unlike him, no one paid me to get that dirty. I did it happily as a labor of love for my first offshore sailboat. I sanded until I was blue in the face, blue all over in fact from the dust of the blue antifouling paint I used. When I was finished sanding, I sneezed blue for three days. Then I put on fresh bottom paint and wore splotches of blue on my hands and face for a while. I got blue again when I wet-sanded off a good portion of the paint I had worked so hard to put on so that I would have a fast racing bottom.

I shudder at the memory. I shudder especially when I see the boatyard workers who now paint my boat looking like space walkers, shrouded in Tyvek suits and hoods, protected by goggles, gas masks, gloves and boots. I shudder at the way—nonchalant, like Humphrey Bogart smoking a cigarette—we handled poison made to kill plants and animals that attempted to attach themselves to our boats.

If we didn't think about ourselves, we certainly didn't think about the rest of the environment, the effect of the poisons we flushed into sewers or allowed to become concentrated in crowded harbors. We were ignorant then; now we're smarter. If we have become in some ways a crybaby society, obsessed with the safety of everything from aspirin bottles to zippers, plastered with warning labels, protected by bureaucrats with satchels of regulations, there are a few good reasons for it, among them the damage that can be done by nonchalant handling of toxic stuff like antifouling paint.

Paint makers now sell us products that no longer contain tin or lead or excessive amounts of solvents but still keep bottoms clean and even come in nice colors. Good laws enacted to protect the water in which we sail have complicated the once simple, if nasty, job of bottom painting. One result is that, increasingly, this is becoming work that boatyards do and amateurs avoid.

Besides keeping sailors and the world in general safer, this pretty much rules out paid captains having to paint their boss's boats and perhaps restores a bit of the glamour to the job. On the other hand, since ostentation is out in the '90s, these pros are less often called captains. Mostly they're known as BMWs (for boat maintenance workers) or even more demeaning initials. So much for the glamour.

In Search of
Vanishing Stability

DO you know your boat's AVS? Did Isabelle Autissier know hers?

Every boat owner probably should. At the very least, sailors ought to talk about AVS, if only because it is one of the most delightful terms to articulate in all of sailing. Not as an acronym or initials, which sound more like a disease than something to do with sailboats, but in its full, mellifluous form.

Angle of Vanishing Stability.

Oh, the elegance of it. It had to be coined by a poet, certainly not an engineer.

I don't know whom to credit for the term, but I'll wager he or she has more than a passing acquaintance with Shakespeare. A person less attuned to the nuances of the language might have come up with Point of Capsize, a jarring term that would be burdened with an unfortunate acronym—POC, or in the plural, POCs or POX.

The Angle of Vanishing Stability is the heeling angle at which a boat capsizes. If a boat's AVS is 120 degrees, it will tip over when it heels beyond that angle.

A lively discussion about AVS is going on in Europe in the wake of the tragicomic events of the Around Alone Race. Which gets us back to Autissier, who became the poster girl for AVS by managing to exceed that magic angle in a mere 25 knots of wind and moderate seas.

We shouldn't hold the dauntless Isabelle accountable for this. It was her boat's designer, Pascal Conq, after all, who gave her an Open Class 60 so unstable that it capsized after an unplanned jibe caused by poor steering by the autopilot. To add insult to injury, the boat then refused to right itself.

This would have been funny—a 60-foot ocean racing boat flipping over in circumstances more typical of a Wednesday night beer can race than an around-the-world epic—if it hadn't happened in the Southern Ocean too far away from civilization for rescue by ship or helicopter. It was a fellow racer, Giovanni Soldini, who came to the rescue of Autissier after she spent a day camping in the overturned hull at latitude 56 degrees south. This splendid act of seamanship turned out to be the high point of a race that, thanks to vanished stability, slipped perilously close to farce when only two of the boats in the 60-foot class were able to finish.

Farce, in fact, is what English television made of the consequences of AVS when it aired a comedy recently that featured sailors, who were competing in an around-the-world race, trapped in an overturned boat. Well, the spectacle of sailboats floating around with their keels sticking up in the air does have a certain Monty Python ring to it.

The proclivity of the Open 60s to tip over and stay that way suggests (none too subtly) that there is a limit to how much can be done to add speed to a monohull designed to race around the world. With multihulls, on the other hand, there may be no limit—the faster they get, the more stable they seem to be. This is ironic in that the rap against multihulls (by monohull adherents) has always been that, because they don't have that big lead thing sticking out of their bottoms, they tend to capsize.

Cats can turn turtle, of course. Not for nothing was the escape hatch in the bottom of the boat invented by catamaran sailors. But the big ocean racing two-hullers, which can carry a beam greater than half of their length, have shown an ability to stay upright in extreme conditions.

The speed and stability of catamarans will be put to an interesting test starting December 31, 2000 in an around-the-world free-for-all called The Race. It has no rules besides some required marks of the course. Participants can sail in whatever they want. Some will opt for very large monohulls. But the most amazing boats will be the catamarans.

We've already seen what Steve Fossett's *PlayStation*, a 105-foot catamaran built for The Race, can do. Recently it broke the 24-hour distance record by sailing 580 miles—that's an average speed faster than 24 knots. *PlayStation*, believe it or not, may be one of the more conservative multihull entries.

On the radical side, Pete Goss' catamaran will be 115 feet long and have a mast on each hull, each supporting a giant windsurferlike sail. Goss says the boat will have a top speed of 40 knots. Will it stay upright? Probably. The boat will be as wide as an Open Class 60-footer is long.

Goss knows something about AVS. On Christmas day in the 1996-97 Vendée Globe Race, the Englishman joined the pantheon of sailing heroes by sailing upwind 160 miles in a nightmarish Southern Ocean storm to rescue a French sailor whose 60-footer had capsized and sunk. Through the ordeal, Goss' 50-foot boat skated on the edge of disaster, but was able to survive numerous near-capsizes, a fact Goss attributes to its canting keel. The boat was designed by Adrian Thompson, who later designed Goss' mega-cat.

Most of us ordinary sailors don't worry about our garden variety, ballasted monohull boats capsizing. We don't have to, because most of us don't sail where the waves are big enough to roll a boat over. But even for boats that stay out of the Southern Ocean, manage to avoid hurricanes and don't enter the Sydney-Hobart Race, the AVS number is a helpful indicator of the ability to stand up to dangerous conditions.

People who know about these things can produce a righting moment curve that reveals the dreaded angle where stability vanishes. A high AVS number, say 140 degrees, indicates plenty of stability and, like a high IQ and a low cholesterol count, comes with bragging rights.

This could present the opportunity to declaim in the yacht club bar, with rhetorical flourish in keeping with the grace of the term, that ... My Angle of Vanishing Stability is superior to yours.

Behold these
Gorgeous Things

THE criteria for beautiful women haven't changed since Eve. Beautiful sailboats are another story.

Hull lines that made boats raving beauties 20 or 30 years ago now seem as odd as the fins on a 1960 Cadillac. Features that would have been considered a sin against nature then make some contemporary sailboats astonishingly good looking.

Or so it seems to this beholder's eye. When I came of age in off-shore sailing, I thought the racer-cruisers designed by Bill Tripp were the most beautiful objects on the water. I got goosebumps looking at a Columbia 50, and once traveled to the Pacific Coast for no other purpose than to sail one.

When I see a Columbia 50 now, I wonder what I was thinking. Almost everything about this hull, except the deep sheerline, seems ridiculously high—the transom, the overall freeboard, the spoon bow that soars to an elevation that could give the bowman a nosebleed. The overhangs are so long that this 50-footer has a waterline length shorter than some of today's 40-footers.

This was the look of sailing speed and power in the 1960s, and it was not an illusion. In its brief glory days, the Columbia 50 was a formidable race winner. What's more, its amazing height served some practical purposes. It made possible a flush deck that was a joy to work on, and provided a voluminous interior.

I still admire those old Tripp designs, and was pleased two

years ago to vote to induct one of them, the Bermuda 40, into the American Sailboat Hall of Fame, but as exemplars of sailing beauty they have given way to a yacht design genre in which, interestingly enough, another Bill Tripp, the late Mr. Tripp's son, is a practitioner, among other designers of IMS racing boats.

As in most things man-made, form follows function in sailboat design, but in the works of these designers of no-compromise racing boats, form seems an accident of function, albeit a happy one. In a retrospective review of an old design by Tripp the elder, yacht designer Bob Perry observed that the hull's voluptuous overhangs seemed to serve no purpose except to please the eye of the designer. In the designs of the present-day Tripp and his peers, every line and curve, every nuance, serve the function of speed. The resulting shapes are spare, economical, even severe, combining features rarely associated with pretty boats—sharp, pinched, plumb bows, nearly straight sheerlines, low, wide sterns. They are gorgeous.

This look has evolved as the standard form for offshore racing boats from 30 to 80 feet long. Length helps. The shorter boats have boxy profiles and other flaws. I once irritated a famous designer by writing that his 36-footer had a "goofy-looking" cabin house. I stand by that assessment, but he shouldn't have taken offense. To comply with IMS accommodation rules, he had no choice but to add a high, light bulb-shaped affair for head-room. As these hull shapes lengthen past 40 feet they acquire a graceful balance, and when they reach maxi-size the IMSers are breathtaking.

Those ubiquitous initials, the shorthand for handicap, have had a lot to do with the way sailboats have looked in the latter half of this century. Today's beauties are influenced by the IMS. The Columbia 50 was a product of the CCA. Boats in between reflected the tortured tenets of the IOR. The IMS boats are the most handsome, no doubt because this rule, unlike its predecessors, does not penalize the pure forms that yield speed and stability.

Standards of beauty for cruising designs that are not ruled by initials have changed too. The Saga 43, for example, a new Bob Perry-designed passage-maker, has a look somewhat derivative of around-the-world race boats. It exudes a sense of its purpose, which is to sail fast through anything anywhere, and therein lies its beauty.

It's conceivable that some years into the future we'll look back on these boats and think they look as odd as the Columbia 50 does now. Only a few sailboat designs, after all, are truly timeless.

What, then, is the most beautiful currently-built sailboat? Without a second's hesitation, I will say it is the Alerion Express, a 28-foot fiberglass version of a daysailer designed by Nathanael G. Herreshoff more than 80 years ago. Its understated lines, all grace and harmony with short overhangs, a conservative sheerline and low stern, yield an uncommonly pretty hull. Beyond that, the Alerion, much in the way of those all-business IMS boats, looks eager and able to sail fast. This perfect wedding of form and function is not just a beauty—it's a timeless beauty.

If a boat can be beautiful, can a boat also be ugly? Or is "ugly sailboat" an oxymoron on the order of "jumbo shrimp?" I've heard it said that almost any boat built of ferrocement in a backyard and every one of those unfortunate boats with exaggerated reverse sheers that were once popular in Britain are ugly. I've heard that said, too, about an unusual sailboat moored near mine, but I wonder.

Less than 20 feet long, the boat is welded together of five sheets of steel with not a single complex curve. On top of this pointed box, that appears to stand higher than the bow of a

Columbia 50, sits a tiny sloop rig swiped from a one-design. The boat's devoted owner uses it far more than do the owners of the sleek craft moored all around it. It is obvious that he derives a tremendous joy from sailing this strange little boat. To him, I'm quite sure, it is beautiful.